Contents

Becoming a writer

The NATIONAL *Writing* PROJECT

Nelson

Thomas Nelson and Sons Ltd
Nelson House   Mayfield Road
Walton-on-Thames   Surrey
KT12 5PL   UK

York Place
Edinburgh
EH1 3JD   UK

Thomas Nelson (Hong Kong) Ltd
Toppan Building 10/F
22A Westlands Road
Quarry Bay   Hong Kong

Distributed in Australia by

Thomas Nelson Australia
480 La Trobe Street
Melbourne   Victoria 3000
and in Sydney, Brisbane, Adelaide and Perth

©SCDC Publications 1989
First published by Thomas Nelson and Sons Ltd 1989

Photographs: A. MacGregor (pp 6, 18, 28, 32, 67, 71, 76, 84, 91)

ISBN 0-17-424113-5
NPN 9 8 7 6 5 4 3 2

Printed and bound in Great Britain by Bell & Bain Ltd, Glasgow

Acknowledgements

Hundreds of teachers and thousands of children have participated in the National Writing Project. They have been supported by many local advisers, members of higher education colleges, parents and others in the community. We cannot name them all, but we would like to acknowledge the commitment of those participants, and trust that these publications represent at least some of their views about classroom practice.

The National Writing Project was set up by the School Curriculum Development Committee. Its three-year Development Phase (1985-1988) directly involved twenty-four local authorities and it was funded jointly by the School Curriculum Development Committee and the LEAs. In 1988, the National Curriculum Council took responsibility for the Project's final implementation year.

Central Project Team (Development Phase 1985-1988)

Pam Czerniewska: Director

Eve Bearne
Barbara Grayson   } Project Officers
John Richmond
Jeremy Tafler

Naomi Baker
Anne Hogan   } Administrators
Judy Phillips

Central Project Team (Implementation Phase 1988-1989)

Jeremy Tafler: Director

Georgina Herring   } Project Officers
Marie Stacey

Rosemary Robertson: Administrator

Steering Committee

Andrew Wilkinson: Chair

Dennis Allen
Peter Andrews
Iain Ball
Douglas Barnes
Eunice Beaumont
Harold Gardiner
Alan Hall
David Halligan
John Johnson
Gulzar Kanji
Keith Kirby
Maggie Maclure
June Thexton
Jenny Taylor
Mike Torbe
Janet White

Local Project Co-ordinators

Avon	Richard Bates
Bedfordshire	Mary Heath
Berkshire	Audrey Gregory
	Barry Pope
Birmingham	Ann Davis
	Sylvia Winchester
Cheshire	Gill Fox
	John Huddart
Cleveland	Margaret Meek
	Joan Sedgewicke
Croydon	Sheila Freeman
	Iain Weir
Dorset	Barbara Tilbrook
	Margaret Wallen
Dudley	Chris Morris
Durham	Dot Yoxall
Gwynedd	Len Jones
	Esyllt Maelor
	Nia Pierce Jones
Hampshire	Robin Culver
	Cath Farrow
	Ann Heslop
	Roger Mulley
Humberside	Sylvia Emerson
ILEA	Helen Savva
Manchester	Helen Henn
	Georgina Herring
Mid Glamorgan	Richard Landy
Newcastle	Jay Mawdsley
Rochdale	Frances Clarke
	Peter Phethean
	Vivienne Rowcroft
SCEA	Stuart Dyke
Sheffield	Sue Horner
Shropshire	Ned Ratcliffe
Somerset	Vernon Casey
	Maisie Foster
	Carole Mason
Staffordshire	Sallyanne Greenwood
Wiltshire	Gill Clarkson
	Sue Dean
	Jo Stone

Introduction

It is always fascinating to watch young children as they learn how to walk, how to talk, how to make sense of their world. Whatever aspect of learning is considered, there is always speculation about how children do it. Is there some innate mechanism controlling development? How much learning is a question of imitating those around them? Are children actively involved in working out the adult systems? Is there a fixed order of development? Do different environments affect the rate and direction of development?

These are key issues about how a child learns, issues which either implicitly or explicitly underlie teaching methods. A classroom, for example, where children spend considerable time copying letters beneath the teacher's clear print runs on assumptions about learning which are very different from those of a classroom where children write independently, inventing letter shapes and spelling. These assumptions rarely surface for close interrogation.

This collection of ideas about writing development in the early years — from age three to seven — takes as its starting point a view of learning in which the child is central. The child is seen as the main agent of development. Through their encounters with different examples, children make sense of literacy practices.

When Paul writes:

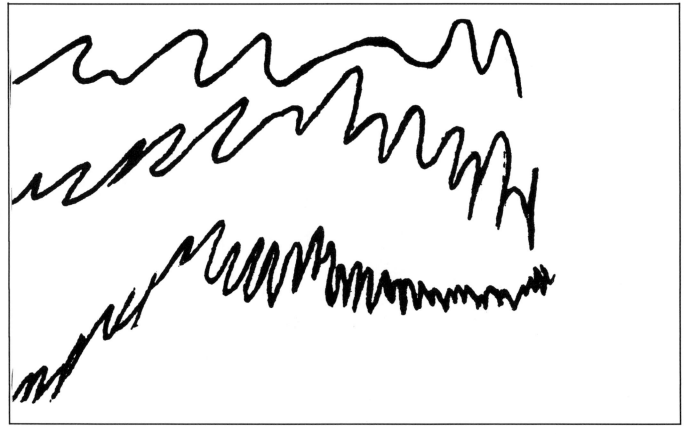

Paul

he is demonstrating his knowledge of English writing: moving the pen from left to right in horizontal lines and adopting a style resembling adult script.

Stacey uses her knowledge of literacy to make a calendar with sections for the days of the week . . .

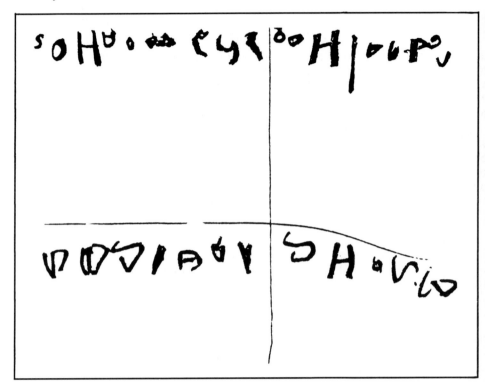

Stacey

. . . while Andrew writes down his rainbow song in appropriately chosen writing. Andrew drew a picture first, and told the teacher that it was a rainbow song. The teacher asked if he would like to write it down. Perhaps because there was already musical notation in the classroom, Andrew chose to write his song in a similar style.

Andrew

Avon Writing Project

These children demonstrate a considerable grasp of what writing can convey, and are clearly engaged in innovative explorations of what they have observed about the literate world around them. As they grow older, their experience of writing will lead to new experiments and further refinements, a process that should continue throughout life.

Although the child is seen to be in the centre of the learning process, it should not be assumed that learning will take place regardless of adult intervention. Such a horticultural model of development — the child's abilities unfolding, affected only slightly by the surrounding soil — fails to reflect the interactive nature of learning. Children learn how writing works through observation of and interaction with the many writers and writing systems around them. Long before they come to school they will have received strong messages about what writing is, what it is for and how it is valued by people around them. They will have developed hypotheses about its usefulness and its uses.

J.S. Bruner reflects this shift in thinking away from 'the solo child mastering the world' towards a social constructivist perspective when he writes:

'I have come increasingly to recognise that most learning in most settings is a communal activity, a sharing of the culture. It is not just that the child must make his knowledge his own, but that he must make it his own in a community of those who share his sense of belonging to a culture. It is this that leads me to emphasise not only discovery and invention but the importance of negotiating and sharing . . .'[1]

On this view, children can be seen not only constructing a view of how writing works, but also constructing a view of themselves as writers. Every nursery or reception class contains children who say they can't write, and children who will happily pick up a pen and write at length, albeit often unintelligibly to an adult eye. Children also develop ideas about what they should write about. Examples of this can be seen in the gender-related preferences of boys and girls: boys tend to adopt more active/violent themes in their stories (transformers, Batman, Incredible Hulk), while girls choose more caring/domestic themes (My Little Pony, fairies, weddings) — tendencies evident in their nursery writing. Thus children, in their pre-school experiences, develop different perceptions of writing and writers, perceptions which need to be recognised and mediated by the teacher, parent and others.

The view of the child as an active participant in learning, gaining control of the adult systems through interaction with other writers and through experience of a range of writing forms and functions, indicates certain directions for the classroom teacher to follow.

The Manchester Writing Project teachers picture the diverse roles of the teacher of writing like this:

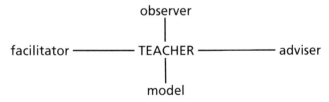

- observing children, noting the experiments they are making with writing and the hypotheses they seem to be drawing about its structure and uses

- observing how children respond to the various classroom writing tasks

- observing the classroom itself and the messages it is transmitting

[1] J.S. Bruner: *Actual Minds, Possible Worlds* (Harvard Educational Press)

- facilitating the child's explorations by creating a literate environment which draws on the child's own cultural and linguistic resources

- facilitating the child's experiences by providing relevant purposes and audiences for writing and ensuring that children experience a full range of literacy activities

- advising the writer by providing a reader-response, giving editorial support when it is asked for and providing an experienced writer's viewpoint

- modelling the writing process by writing for and alongside the children

- modelling by inviting writers into the classroom: parents, older children, published authors

- modelling by giving access to different forms of writing in all subject areas

- supporting the writer through the provision of as many resources as possible: pens, felt-tip pens, note pads, class books, zig-zag books, magnetic letters, word processors, typewriters . . . and more

The teacher, with these diverse roles, intervenes in the child's learning not so much by specific instruction (though that might be appropriate) but through the careful structuring of the context such that children see literacy as relevant and satisfying, and as something over which they have control.

The diagram below attempts to summarise the plan for action suggested by this view of writing development.

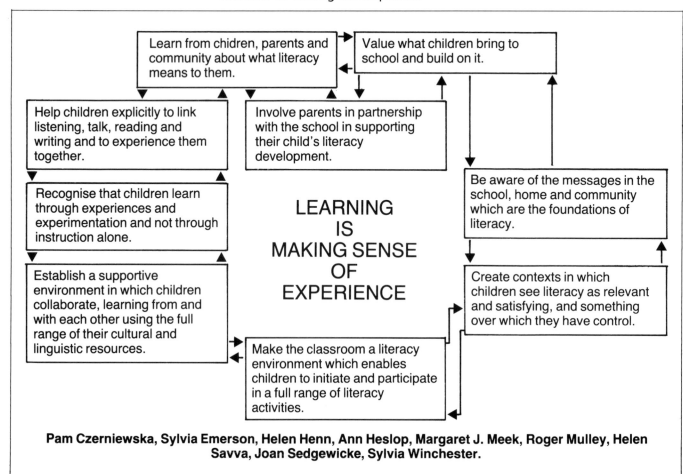

Pam Czerniewska, Sylvia Emerson, Helen Henn, Ann Heslop, Margaret J. Meek, Roger Mulley, Helen Savva, Joan Sedgewicke, Sylvia Winchester.

There are three sections in this pack, each of which is related to the others but can be read and discussed separately.

Section One looks at the writer's community outside the school, examining the pre-school experiences children may have and the value they may place on writing before they begin formal learning. The role of parents receives particular attention, with examples of how home-school links can be established and promoted.

Section Two focuses on the writer's environment inside school, taking up the central issue of the child's control over what is learned. There are many examples of the support and facilitation given by teachers to promote a child's development of writing, from the provision of a writing centre to strategies that encourage planning and drafting.

Section Three observes the development of individual children, providing examples of writing which demonstrate the unique ways in which children experiment with new forms, practise what they already know and try to make sense of the literacy environment in which they live. At the end of this section some controversial issues are directly addressed: What about spelling? Will parents accept new approaches? How can development be recorded?

The teachers whose work is included here were writing as part of their own reflective process and many of the case studies were written at the beginning of their involvement in the Project. They do not constitute conclusions or solutions. Many teachers have used their initial exploratory writing as the basis of more penetrating analysis, looking, for example, at fundamental issues of social stereotyping, gender, and multicultural education.

No collection of materials about such a large area as this can hope to be comprehensive. This pack aims, in a very modest fashion, to raise a few issues and reflect teachers' different starting points, in the hope that from this other teachers will be able to reflect on their own practices.

Consultative Group

Pam Czerniewska
Sylvia Emerson
Ann Heslop
Carole Mason
Margaret J. Meek
Roger Mulley
Joan Sedgewicke
Jo Stone

With thanks to the many others who contributed, in particular National Writing Project co-ordinators: Helen Henn, Georgina Herring, Jay Mawdsley, Helen Savva, Sylvia Winchester and Dot Yoxall.

Thanks, too, to Vivienne Miller and Marion Murray from Dorset, and to all the other teachers involved in trialling groups around the country, particularly those of Oldham, Northamptonshire and Cambridgeshire, many of whose comments are included in the text.

1 The writer's community

When do children learn to write? What affects that learning? What effects will early experiences of writing have on later development? What role do parents, teachers and others play?

These questions form the starting point for our reflections on the writing development of young children. Children are learning about writing and writers from their very early days. When a fifteen-month-old child writes:

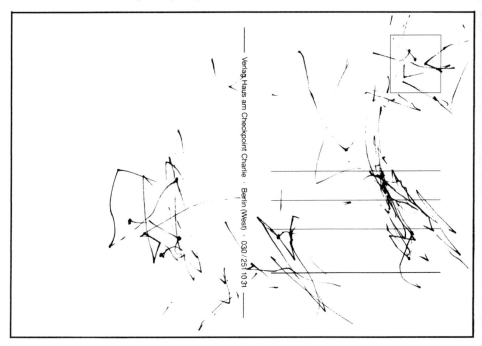

Alexandra

she demonstrates her knowledge of the place of writing in her culture: this is what people around her do. As she gains more experience, her experiments with writing will develop, slowly moving closer to the adult models around her.

What those experiences are, how they are interpreted by children and how they can be mediated by parents, teachers and those around them will be the focus of this section. By starting outside the classroom we are emphasising that the foundations of literacy rest on the messages not only in the school but also in the home and community.

What are the child's literacy experiences in the home, the street, the classroom? The obvious answer is that, in this society, children live in a print-rich world. It is full of writing: signs, posters, cards, newspapers, T-shirts and so on. It is also full of writers: people writing cheques, signing cards, sending letters, writing out lists, filling in forms and more.

Children clearly learn from these experiences of print in the very early years. Their initial attempts at writing will have recognisable writing characteristics and by nursery age, children can easily demonstrate their awareness of certain characteristics of print and their memory of the print around them. The four-year-old in a Manchester nursery who produced *'AIDS DON'T DIE OF IGNORENCE'* (*sic*) provides a telling example. He may not have understood the message, but he knew which bits of the media campaign to memorise (almost correctly) and that it was an important message.

Young children do not merely absorb the writing around them. They are actively engaged in finding out what adults write about and for what purpose, and trying to match their writing behaviour to this. They learn many surprising details. For example, when a nursery teacher provides a range of forms, pads and paper, the children's invented writing will generally be adapted in some way to suit the purpose. For instance, a pre-schooler's signature will be very different from her telephone message.

I was standing at the wallchart making a list for Soft Play, and as I read out the list to the children, Alison came to me and asked, 'Can I go to Soft Play?' I replied that she wasn't on the list this week. Alison walked away, reappearing several minutes later with a piece of paper, saying, 'Miss Huart, I can go to Soft Play because I'm on the list. Look!'

Some examples from Newcastle nurseries further illustrate how young children learn about the significance of writing.

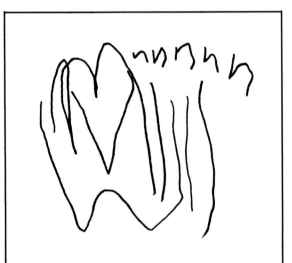

Alison

Michelle Huart, Nursery, Westgate Hill Infants

Clare (three years, seven months) was asked, *'Would you like me to write your name on the paper?'* She pointed to the top right-hand corner and replied, *'No, look, I've done it.'* She had recently been talking about *C* for *Clare* and had written what was clearly her name, with *C* at the beginning, with the whole word of approximately the right length and with the definite look of a word.

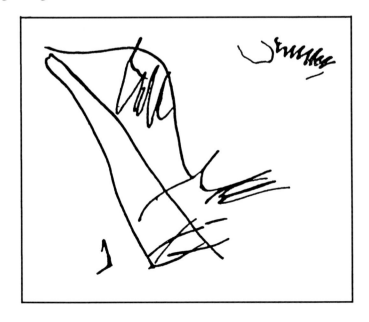

Clare

Alexander (four years, two months) was writing a letter to Santa. He wrote it using mainly upper case letters from his name — *E*s, *A*s and *N*s.

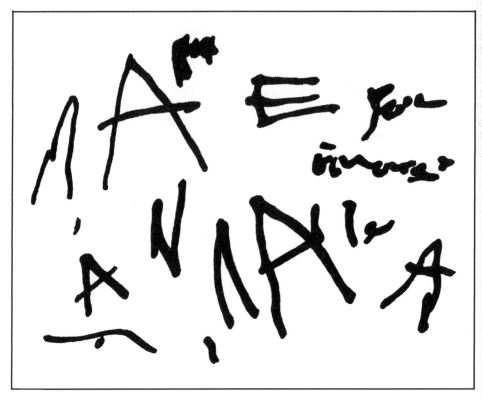

Alexander

Tina Watson, Nursery, Tyneview Primary School

Children are constantly trying to make sense of what is going on around them. This includes trying to work out how the writing system is organised and coming to conclusions which will often be revised. In Section Three there are further examples of young children's strategies to represent the adult writing system, which show how much children do manage to achieve in the early years without formal instruction.

An assumption that underlies much of the current Infant curriculum is that writing is taught once children enter school. Writing thus contrasts with oral language which, it is often said, is learned at home. Writing is considered a second-order activity, superimposed on the primary skill of talking.

The difficulty with such an assumption is that it produces the view that the child spends the pre-school years ignoring all the print around him/her. It may also create the impression in children that the writing that they meet in school is different in some way from the writing outside the classroom.

Evidence of pre-schoolers' writing experiments calls for a reassessment of the writing provision in the classroom. Does it provide opportunities for children to demonstrate all that they know about the writing community? Are there message pads by the phone? Does the shop have order books and cheques? Do the walls have a range of different types of print? Do the children see many writers other than other children? In Section Two these points are examined further.

Shared understandings

As well as working out the significant characteristics of writing systems, children will also be developing a view of themselves as writers. A depressing finding is that whereas most children enter school saying, *'I can write'*, after a short time many of these will have decided that they cannot write. Their perceptions of writing — what it's for and who is able to do it — will be determined in part at least by the way the teacher describes a task, responds to a piece of writing and demonstrates the value placed on particular types of writing. To find out just what types of message have been conveyed to children, many teachers have interviewed their class, asking questions such as, *'What's important about writing?'* *'What makes a piece of writing good?'* *'Will you write when you're older?'*

Are you a good writer?

Sort of!   *Bad – my spellings are wrong*

No – untidy!   *Nearly – I would be much better if I was faster*

Yes – neat! I get the right words in my head and spell them wrong   *Yes – I can spell hard words*

Yes and no – not really sure   *No – too scribbly*

No – I go under the lines   *Yes, because I use more than one piece of paper when writing stories*

Some children in the schools in the Durham project were asked about writing. Frequently, children's perceptions of why they wrote did not match the teacher's, and their answers provided the basis of much discussion in staffrooms.

What is the most difficult part?

Writing with a small pencil – makes your hand ache   *Getting ideas*

Making up your own story   *Doing very hard words*

Thinking about it   *To get the pieces to match properly*

What is the easiest part?

Sums

Things you can spell

When you can choose what to write

Big pencils

When you get help

When you do the end part

The beginning

What do you like to write least of all?

Something you don't know very much about

Poems – it's hard to think of words that rhyme

Copying the blackboard

Long words

Filling in missing words

Some books are hard

Why do we learn to write?

So we can read

To fill in forms

Helps us to spell

So we can communicate with each other

So you will know what to write in the big school

So we are ready to go in the Juniors

To write letters when you grow up

To write stories for teachers

To write reports when you grow up

Often the superficial features of writing — neatness, presentation, correct spelling — were considered to be most important, and were used by children to assess whether writing was good and whether the writer was successful. In general, writing was not considered as a means of learning, as a way of reaching new understanding or of gaining new knowledge, but as a means of recording what has been told or read.

The majority of children considered writing to be very important but found it more difficult to say why. They thought that writing was preparation for work and for the unknown — the Juniors, the big school, being grown up. It seemed that the purpose of writing *here and now* was not considered.

Of course, literacy has been associated with work for the last hundred years but, as M. Spencer points out, literacy is less clear in its function. She stresses the need to provide children with an understanding of the complex 'literacies' that surround them.

'In helping children to learn to read we, as teachers, tend to concentrate on the task in hand according to our view of it, leaving to the learners, when they progress beyond our care, the adaptation to its functions in society of what we helped them to learn.' [2]

A six-year-old in Mary Chamberlain's class in Newcastle wrote:

what I think about writing
Some times when I write I dont do
long storys. Because ~~it get~~ my hands
get read out. I like Writing storys.
And (tired) Poems at home because there
Was nothing els to do. But I had to
get the paper first Sometimes readin
-g helps me write. Because I rememb
-er Words from books. My writing get
-s better evrey school day. Sometimes
at home I do exciting storys. But Some
times I do to many ands. So I read
what I rit first. I dont Like people
reading my writing.

Zoë - Age 6

[2] M. Spencer: 'Emergent literacies: a site for analysis' from *Language Arts 63 No. 5*

Studies of children's perceptions of writing and their approaches to writing tasks demonstrate that we need to see what understandings of literacy a child has developed, with whom such understandings are shared, and whether there is a mismatch in their interpretation of writing with that of the school. Learning cannot take place effectively without shared understanding of how the learner behaves and the nature of the learning task. To discover the child's understandings involves looking at the child not only in the classroom but also in interaction at home.

Shared practice

How curious it must seem to a child beginning school if so many of his/her early experiments with print are not recognised and understood by the adults in class. Confusion must surely occur if what was accepted as writing at home is not considered writing at school, or *vice versa.* It is a question of expectations. Teachers, parents and children will all have developed a set of expectations about how each group should behave and react. Children entering school for the first time will have different expectations. One child will write pages of his/her own particular marks, assured of the value of this 'writing' to the reader; another child will be reluctant to write and want every spelling to be supplied by the teacher. The teacher will have his/her own expectations which may support only one group of children. if there is a mismatch of expectations, at best a sense of frustration will develop, at worst a sense of failure.

In order to find out about the expectations of parents, teachers in Manchester sent a questionnaire to all parents of nursery and reception children in twelve schools.

The questionnaire dealt with the following areas:

- their own writing experiences as children, at home and at school
- why they thought writing was important
- what role they thought the school should adopt to help develop writing
- what role they thought they should adopt to help develop writing
- what writing they themselves did at home
- what further information they would like about the school's writing policy

Please indicate how important you think each of the following is, by ticking the appropriate box:

	very important	important	average	not important	trivial
To communicate to others					
To spell correctly					
To learn to read					
To cope with school work					
To get a job					

Do you feel that schools spend enough time on the teaching of writing?

Yes   Unsure   No   (please tick)

There were over four hundred replies demonstrating a diverse set of views. Two questions provided particularly illuminative responses. One concerned the help parents gave to prepare their children for writing. Here, the responses reflected an emphasis on getting it right. For example:

'He asks how to spell words e.g. ''dinosaur'', ''train'', ''rocket'' etc. I shout out the first letter, he writes it down and so on. I also write down a word and he copies it.'

'Write words in printed roundhand for her to copy for cards, letters etc. Hold or guide her hand while she writes. She wrote a letter to Father Christmas which she dictated and then we looked up every letter which we copied from a book. It was agony.'

Another question, however, asked about the writing activities parents did with their children, and here a great range of supportive work was mentioned: joint writing of shopping lists; the child adding her postscript to letters; designing and sending greeting cards, and so on.

There seemed to be two types of help being given: the formal instructional sort perhaps based on a view of school expectations, and the informal sort derived from everyday writing needs. Many parents have not always recognised the value of the latter.

About three-quarters of the parents said they would like to know more about the school policy on learning to write, a finding to which Project schools were able to respond.

Informal partnership

Many teachers fear, understandably, that any change from a traditional way of teaching writing will meet with parental anxiety or opposition. However, accounts from teachers around the country suggest that when parents and teachers begin to talk about writing and its importance for learning, about themselves as writers, and about their children's writing development, a new, jointly constructed approach to writing can develop.

In schools which welcome parents into classrooms regularly, it is easy to talk with them about children's work and how it develops. Parents read notices, hear children and teachers talking about their work together, talk with staff and, above all, can become involved themselves, observing what children do and say.

In such schools, a passing remark can often stimulate a parent into looking at his/her own child's work with a more sympathetic and informed eye. It can help him/her to see ways in which (s)he too can be involved in those learning processes which are sometimes regarded as 'the school's business'.

Informed conversations

Such a partnership must be beneficial to our children, supporting them as they learn, develop new ideas and gain confidence in their ability to express meaning in writing. The examples below are drawn from several schools where informal — but informed — talk about children's writing is actively promoted.

Mark, at four-and-a-half years old, was fascinated by letters and their shapes. He spent a lot of time making letter patterns: in different colours, with paint, when he was drawing, on the clay table. One day he made a shopping list to give to someone in the nursery who had made a shop with big blocks. The list looked like this:

Mark

This was the beginning of a whole new way of using letters. Although he still made patterns with letters, the patterns usually looked very much like lists, with each item written as a series of the same letter in different colours. He wrote messages of one kind and another — in the home corner, as telephone messages, notes for the milkman and, above all, shopping lists.

One day, his teacher found this list left behind at the end of the session:

Mark

Next day, she asked Mark what it said. *'Bread, potatoes, eggs, rice crispies, marge, baked beans'* — of course!

When his mum saw this, she was not in the least surprised. *'Oh yes,'* she said. *'He's always helping me make lists at home.'* When he was younger she had often asked him to look in the cupboards to see if they needed to buy various items, and he would regularly take part in the compilation of shopping lists.

Steven spent a lot of his later time in the nursery drawing and writing, making complex maps, plans and designs. He used rulers and incorporated letters and numerals into his work, usually in appropriate places.

Steven

A map to my nan's house in Scotland

His mother said that they didn't *'bother with writing much with him'* and he didn't *'do this kind of work at home'.* One day, his father came to collect him from nursery and the teacher showed him some of Steven's work. He said, *'That's just what I do! Well — look at that! I always do work up in the bedroom when I have to bring it home, and I didn't think he was taking any notice of it. Yes, he was interested in the maps when we went on holiday, but that's ages ago. Fancy him remembering.'*

One day, Christopher was observed writing with his friend in the nursery office. He had several sheets of paper folded together as a book and, when he had completed three pages of text, he also found and folded a sheet of coloured paper.

As he carried his book, under his arm, from one area to another, I asked if he would read it to me. Christopher explained that he had made a newspaper and the pink folder was the colour supplement.

When his mother arrived, Christopher was still carrying his newspaper, and it was suggested that he should bring it back to school the next day to complete it if he wanted to.

Christopher

His mother was pleased to hear that I thought this paper was very unusual — I'd never seen a newspaper written by a four-year-old before! The next day, she reported what had happened at home.

The other members of Christopher's family had valued his newspaper; his father had asked him to look in his paper for times of television programmes, and his elder brother wanted to look at the football page.

Christopher explained that his paper wasn't finished yet, and so it travelled to and from school for about a week. His mother reported how everyone at home read it every night and noted new articles — but Christopher would not translate his writing.

At last, he read it to me — and then it stayed at home.

Most parents talked about materials, and there was some concern about the cost of these and the problems of children writing in inappropriate places. (The wallpaper seemed a popular choice.) Some felt that writing and associated skills would come later. *'He'll settle down to it when he's ready'* expressed a common view. There was talk about teaching a child to write her name, although this was often followed by concern that parents didn't know how to teach such skills properly and might *'mess things up'* at school.

Discussion led the parents to realise that they did indeed provide their young children with many and varied opportunities for developing their knowledge about the ways the written/printed word carries messages. Further conversations between parents and teachers demonstrated the value of shifting attention away from the child's struggles with the conventions of spelling and letter formation, and towards his/her ability to convey messages. From this new focus, many ways of supporting the writing environment of home and of school emerged.

Cleveland Writing Project

One teacher asked the parents of some of her reception children to tell her about any writing experiences their children had enjoyed at home, before starting school.

One Infant teacher overcame initial hesitations and reservations by building on existing forms of contact.

Parents write too

Talking with parents about writing can stem naturally from casual conversations about policies and practices. For many parents, it's one step on from this to becoming directly involved in classroom activities by engaging in the writing itself. Fears about their own abilities, about the lack of time, about the usefulness of their writing can all be dispelled in a variety of partnership activities.

However was I going to get the parents involved in writing? These parents were not people who would normally write for their children, although they had always been interested in their children's progress and had co-operated with me in other aspects of school life. As I was teaching their children for the second year in succession, we knew each other fairly well and a good relationship had already been formed.

But now I had to experiment with something new. I wondered how I would have felt, as a parent, if I had been asked to write with or for my own children. I know I should have felt very inadequate and absolutely terrified! And yet here am I, contemplating asking parents to do just this, when some of them do not even speak, let alone write, English as a first language.

We started to share reading books in class and we wanted the parents to join us. A book chosen by each child together with a 'contact book' was taken home. The children told their parents that they were to write comments in these books whenever they were brought home. And so it started — slowly at first, and the comments were brief: *'She read very well.' 'He is getting good.'*

As the weeks passed, the remarks became more comprehensive: *'We both enjoyed reading this book, I am very pleased with the way Darren's reading is coming along.'*

'This was a nice book with good stories, not hard and not too easy for Nicola to read, I must say how pleased I am that Nicola's reading seems to improve with every book she reads. And by being allowed to bring these books home, it has encouraged her to want to read.'

This was all very encouraging. The contact books became firmly established, and we felt that this parental involvement in writing could be widened.

'Food' was our topic for that Autumn Term. Having baked English bread in school, we thought about cooking food from other countries. Half of the children in my class had their roots in India, Pakistan, Germany or the Caribbean. An Indian mum was approached, and she willingly agreed to come into school to cook *parathas* with us. From this activity some writing emerged: everyone contributed to a book about *parathas*. Our mum wrote for the children about her pleasure in sharing this new experience with her daughter's class.

On another occasion we talked about our parents in class discussion. We talked about what they did and where they lived when they were young children. We wanted them to come into school and write with us, but family commitments prevented most of them from doing so. Only one parent was able to come into the class and write with her child. I suggested that anyone who wanted to could have a special book to take home. Any member of the child's family could write in it, draw pictures, or make some kind of personal contribution.

At first the parents were hesitant, and some came to see me to ask what they had to do. However, because of the good relationship that existed already, several parents agreed to write at home.

We called our books 'Home Activity Books'. Sometimes a child would write a story or draw a special picture. I always commented on whatever was produced and praised it. I usually wrote a brief personal reply. This method of communication proved very valuable and popular. Gradually, parents began to write. They started to overcome their self-consciousness and to write spontaneously. On every occasion, I believe my follow-up remarks or letters to them were greatly appreciated and necessary. They formed a link between home and school, although they were time-consuming to do. Each contribution was so individual, and humour often flowed between us.

The titles and topics varied. Themes included a football match; a spooky story; animal stories; a Sport's Day story; life in Kingston, Jamaica; school in Germany, Pakistan and India; life in a boys' prep school; a French holiday; Windsor Safari Park; Diwali celebrations; Easter, Easter eggs and Easter flowers; Eid; starting school. It was lovely to receive contributions in Urdu, Hindi, Gujarati and German. The Urdu was translated into English for us by our Urdu-speaking English Second Language member of staff. The parents who wrote in other languages were bilingual so we had English versions as well. On one occasion, the mother wrote in Hindi and the father wrote the same story in English.

Our Home Activity Books are full of a rich mixture of cultures. They contain photos, puzzles, pictures, letters and stories written by children, parents and teachers. Whenever the books were returned to school, we shared the contents together. It was at this point that real pleasure was experienced by the children. Everyone was keen to look at and share all the books. If a parent had written a story I would usually be asked to read it aloud. Sometimes a child would read, and applause often followed! Perhaps the most rewarding time came when a parent's story was the one chosen to be read at storytime. This happened frequently, and everyone would listen enthusiastically time and time again. The expression of happiness on the face of the author's child was a joy to behold.

Towards the end of the school year, our Home Activity Books began to be cross-curricular. Mathematical problems and illustrations started to appear, and I view this as a positive development.

Mavis Musset, Elmwood Infant School, Croydon

Involving the community

Ideas for parental and community involvement range from the modest to the more ambitious. At the ambitious end are newspaper or bookmaking projects in which parents, teacher, children and others write together. Such activities involve organisation and planning, not only to find space for the writers but also to prepare parents for the work involved.

The following account demonstrates how the community can be involved.

Parental involvement has long been a concern in our school, in both social and academic activities. Having considered ourselves successful in the former, we were aware of a lack of success in the latter. We had little parental involvement in the classroom, although parents were happy to support their children and the teacher in other ways, such as reading with a child at home.

The National Writing Project has highlighted the desirability of home-school partnerships in writing, and we began to explore ways in which we could use the parents and the community to provide writing models for our children.

We began by setting up a Community Notice-board in the school entrance hall. This provided opportunities for parents, children, school staff and other members of the local community to write and display local news items (new babies were a favourite announcement); school and community events or facilities; notices about articles wanted or for sale. Children and parents (illustrators and scribes respectively) described events that had taken place; a 'recipe and household tips' corner was established; letter exchanges took place. The notice-board has become a focus of interest and a valuable resource for everyone who gathers in the entrance hall.

With the notice-board well established, we looked for ways to extend the idea. A community magazine was suggested. A local community arts group agreed to print the magazine on a 'materials only' costing, provided that we could supply the human resources. There seemed no reason for holding back, and so we organised a writing week for the whole school, which would culminate in the publication of the magazine.

We set up an editorial office, equipped with typewriters, editorial notice-boards, paper, pens, pencils and other stationery, and as many adults as we could muster. Children would either submit handwritten copy to be typed, or type their own work. In-trays with labels for categories such as 'sport', 'news', 'travel', 'families', 'pets', 'stories' and, inevitably, 'jokes', were set out to receive contributions. We were ready to go.

Invitations to join us in our writing week had already been sent out to parents, school advisers and other friends of the school, and the Writing Project co-ordinators were planning to come in for most of the week. Monday dawned with the children in a state of high excitement.

The teachers persuaded some of the parents to stay with their children for an hour or so to get them started on their articles and stories for the magazine. The editorial office was soon a hive of industry with expert and inexpert fingers clattering away on the typewriters; the word processors in the classrooms hummed. Adults arrived, looked, talked, wrote. Teachers tore their hair out and wrote. Kitchen staff popped in to have a look, stayed and wrote. The caretaker took a break and wrote. Parents came to help with the typing and wrote. Mums in the community English class wrote. The children wrote and wrote and wrote. They wrote alone, they wrote with a friend; family groups (adults included) wrote family

Families

Shastra Has A Busy Life.

My father, Manga Khan, came to England in 1960. He worked in England for some years and then went back to Pakistan. He got married in Pakistan and his wife (my mother) came to England in 1964. In 1965 my sister was born. I have five brothers and one sister. I am fourth eldest, I was born in 1968. I grew up in Middlesbrough and went to Victoria Road Primary School and then to King's Manor Secondary School. When I left school in 1985 I got engaged to my cousin who lived in Pakistan. I had seen a photograph of my fiancée. I went to Pakistan for the first time to meet my cousin. I stayed there for seven weeks. When my fiancée got his visa to come to England, we both came back together. First we got married in the registry office then we had two big parties in the Mosque.
I have been married for nine months. Before I got married I was on a Y.T.S. scheme, doing clerical work. Now I am working in Breckon Hill Primary School as a bilingual assistant in the nursery and as a dinner nanny.

نام: شاستہ اختر
تاریخ پیدائش: 19.19.68
عمر: اٹھارہ سال
مقام پیدائش: مڈلزبرو، انگلینڈ
مقام: مڈلزبرو

The Khazir family with me. Shabana

histories. They wrote in English, in Urdu, in Turkish and in Bengali. They wrote by hand, they dictated, they typed, they word processed. They wrote in the nursery, in the classrooms, in the hall, in the 'quiet rooms' and in the office. So much paper, so many words, such a good reason for writing.

The problems came when we had to decide what was to go into the magazine and what was to be discarded. After much heart searching, the 'editorial board' arrived at a selection which represented all the age groups involved. We had to omit so much good material that we decided that the work not included in the magazine would be mounted and displayed in the school hall. Parents and children would be invited to look at this exhibition, so that equal value would be placed on all the writing.

During the following week small groups of children and teachers went to the community arts hall and were shown how to set up pages, to cut and stick, to box and display the writing to its best advantage. Several tubes of Pritt later, the layout was complete. They were then shown how the printing was to be done and there was much excitement as the pages began to roll off the press — twenty-two pages in all. The children's pride in the finished product was enormous! Copies were quickly distributed and avidly read, and more copies were requested. The Breckon Hill Community Magazine was launched.

At a staff meeting a couple of weeks later the staff were asked for a realistic evaluation of the writing week. Having generally agreed that the product was excellent, they were now asked to focus on the process, on the involvement of parents and other adults, and on the attitudes of the children.

They agreed that it would have helped if the whole staff had been involved in the planning. This had been undertaken by the Writing Project co-ordinator, the head teacher and one other member of staff. Although planning sheets had been displayed in the staff room, there were still some misunderstandings that could have been avoided if all the staff had been involved right from the start.

One teacher reported a feeling of being overwhelmed by the needs of the children once the initial drafts had been produced and help was requested in checking and polishing. If we ever repeated this exercise, we would try to ensure that each teacher had at least one other adult (preferably a parent) working alongside him/her at all times.

The reaction of the parents had generally been very positive. Many parents had come happily into school to work alongside their children, to write with them and to write themselves. This had raised the profile of writing in the children's eyes, but it had also led to an appreciation of the writing process from the child's point of view.

The head teacher had felt happy to waylay parents who were in the school and bully them into coming to the writing week, because there was a specific purpose in doing so. She also felt that parental response had been very positive for the same reason. It had been particularly pleasing to see the involvement of the Asian parents, many of whom had written in Urdu about their family histories, their countries of origin and their favourite recipes. One of the mothers had enjoyed herself so much that she was now coming in to work in the classroom on a regular basis.

The children's attitudes had been very positive indeed. There was a great eagerness to write, even in those who had previously been the most reluctant writers. They obviously saw more purpose in the task than simply writing in their exercise books or displaying work on the wall. Although, initially, some children asked for suggestions, by the end of the week they were producing their own reasons for writing and were happily working collaboratively as well as individually.

It was generally agreed that this had been an occasion when technology came into its own. It was so much easier for children to get a professional-looking result on a word processor than on a typewriter. It was suggested that another time we would borrow word processors for the children and leave the typewriters for the parents and other adults.

The teachers said that the week had been enjoyable, valuable and definitely worth repeating.

The children said, *'When can we write another magazine?'*

Joan Sedgewicke, Cleveland Writing Project Co-ordinator and Breckon Hill Primary School, Cleveland

The production of a community newspaper in this school began to reach beyond parents to others in the community. There are opportunities to make specific links with the writing community, in particular: shopkeepers, business people, shoppers and senior citizens are all people who write and are written to. The local community provides a rich resource for writing and has a place within the classroom. Further examples of partnerships between the school and the community can be found in the following Theme Packs: *Audiences for Writing; Writing Partnerships 1: home, school and community; Writing Partnerships 2: school, community and the workplace.*

This section has done no more than to provide a few snapshots of the young writer's community; the expectations children, teachers and parents have for writing development; and ways in which such expectations can be shared and built upon. In the next section we will be looking explicitly at the classroom to see how that can become a place which promotes and supports literacy.

2 The writer's environment

Parents and teachers have observed and begun to understand the wealth of literacy events which children experience in their first five years. They bring all this with them into the classroom, and so it is the responsibility of the teacher to provide an environment that will move the child enthusiastically, creatively and systematically forward towards the adult writing system.

In this section we address some key questions about the writer's environment in the school:

- When and where does it happen?
- Who is it for?
- Why do they do it?
- What do they do it with?
- How do they do it?
- Who owns the writing?
- What happens to it?
- Who else is involved?
- What about reading and talking?

They are questions about the relationship between the child, language, and the learning context. At their heart is a fundamental assumption that children learn most effectively when they have involvement in and responsibility for that learning.

Images of print

From the very beginning, the literacy context established by the teacher has a profound influence on the writing achieved by his/her pupils. The classroom is the place where they will probably do most of their writing in the early years, and it will provide a foundation for the attitudes they develop about writing and about themselves as writers. How the classroom is organised, what tasks are introduced, what resources are available: a teacher's policy on all these issues contains assumptions, which need to be considered, about writing development. What, for example, is assumed about the writing process if thirty children have to share three rubbers? What messages are implied in a classroom where only the teacher's writing is on the wall? What view of writing will develop if all writing is done in the same exercise book and for the teacher's eyes only?

Some nursery and reception teachers in Manchester reflected on the images of print in their classrooms, using as a starting point 'The survey of displayed literacy indicators'.[3]

Among the questions asked were:

- Are there timetables, announcements, notices, labels, charts?
- Are they written by the children?
- How much child-written or child-dictated work is there? How old is it? Who displayed it?
- Does the imaginative play area have relevant and accessible literacy materials such as pads, order forms, cheques and appointment books?

[3] N. Hall: *The Emergence of Literacy* (Hodder & Stoughton) 1987, adapted from Loughlin, Cole and Sheehan 1983

- Do children initiate activities involving magazines, cookery books, lists, food labels, posters, etc? Who brings in the materials?
- Are there spaces for writing and reading? When are they used?
- How many non-reading scheme books are there? Who displayed them? Are there comics and newspapers in the library corner? Who selected them?
- Are there supplies of pens, paper, envelopes, typewriters? How accessible are they?

The teachers' responses included the following observations.

When I looked at my classroom in terms of environmental print it was glaringly obvious that I used exclusively adult, mainly lower case print. Even the children's own trays were labelled by me. This was the first change I had to make. All children now write their own names in whatever way they can. They often write labels for their own displayed work, and sometimes do the mounting as well.

I was:

- appalled at the lack of environmental print (not including books)
- aware that all the written display material was teacher-produced and all the same

Having looked around the classroom I discovered that most of the writing was mine; in fact, it was all mine. Lots of it was above children's eye level, although it was aimed at them.

My classroom was full of labels and written instructions, but I was suddenly aware that they were for my benefit as a teacher, and they were what *should* be there; they 'looked right'. The children had no sense of ownership and so the writing was of little value.

Though there is a commitment in the nursery to provide a variety of forms of print, it was evident when examining our current provision of so-called 'displayed literacy' that more examples of non-school writing models were necessary.

Teachers' comments

'Physical limitations were cited as a problem for teachers trying to display more work at child level. Display areas in many schools are high up on the walls; work at child level does tend to become tatty quickly. One school in the group, however, was having special display boards mounted at child height.'

'A point we raised was the question of how much print should be in minority languages. We also felt we had to demonstrate to the children that we valued and respected their language and culture by commenting on the different scripts and styles, rather than simply displaying lots of captions from different languages with no comments made.'

When and where does it happen?

A *place to write*

Pleasing the teacher is something which most reception children want to do, and there was a lot of that going on in my classroom, but what would it be like if the children pleased themselves? The 'writing table' would be a testing ground.

It was made to look as attractive as possible, with paper in a variety of different sizes, colours and shapes. There were pencils, crayons, pens, chalks and charcoal. A bold label announced *'This is our writing table'*.

I introduced the idea to the children by saying that it was an area where they could choose to go to write anything they liked. They could help each other or write on their own. They could share their writing or keep it to themselves. They could write lists, stories, letters, signs, directions, poems — it was their choice.

The writing table was an immediate success with most of the children, although a few did not choose to use it. Using gentle persuasion I encouraged these children to try out the idea. Their initial reactions were, *'But I can't write'*. They needed a lot of reassurance and help. Perhaps I should have shown them examples of other people's writing, including my own. Maybe just sitting and writing with them would have helped; but I tried a different tack. We played a game where they pretended to be writers and we called it 'play writing'. They took their courage in both hands and began to write and draw. One child repeated the full stop *ad infinitum* and was very pleased with himself.

During the first week, every child chose to spend some time at the writing table, although some were keener than others. I then tried allotting group time for the activity. This has been successful, as the less motivated children are swept along with the enthusiasm of the others. Whichever way the writing table is used, I think it is important that its availability is made clear to the children.

I was anxious that the writing table should have lasting value for the children, rather than being simply a novelty. I used the following methods to create a sense of audience and purpose:

1 Children came together in small groups to see each others' work. They either read their own work aloud or asked me to read it. The others usually responded by asking questions, clapping, and pointing out features of the writing that they particularly liked.

2 Some special pieces of writing were shown to other classes, the head teacher, or parents.

3 Books were written and illustrated by the children, and used in class alongside the printed books. A box to house all the children's stories was decorated and suitably labelled.

4 Letters, messages and drawings were sent to my daughter (whom the children know) at university. Her replies were read to and by the children.

5 Drafts undertaken at the writing table were written up in a special book. The children kept these books and could take them home.

6 Children worked with a friend from an early point.

7 Cards and drawings were made and given to friends in the school.

8 I would act as scribe, writing down stories which the children dictated. When the stories were read to other members of the class, the children enjoyed pointing out whose ideas had been used.

Sheila Taylor, Lord's Hill First School, Southampton, Hampshire

One reception teacher thought seriously about the environment in her classroom and decided to provide a 'writing table'.

In this classroom in Cleveland, children responded to the provision made in the 'writing centre' by making little books.

Small beginnings

Initially:

- There was an enormously keen response, with children and writing spilling over on to surrounding tables.

- The classroom was littered with little story books.

- Children wrote about subjects not often seen at school — transformers, Knight Rider etc. The subject matter was often loosely based on television programmes.

- Many little books were wasted — half-finished, and then abandoned.

- Letters home were very popular, usually describing school activities and sending loving messages e.g. *'Dear Mam, I luv you. Sarah.'*

- 'Thank you' letters and requests to Santa were popular.

- Younger children experimented with the little book form, often writing single-page pieces rather than a continuous story.

Later:

- The stream of stories was unabated, but began to reflect more of what was happening in the classroom and the school, e.g. witches at Halloween, *The Little Fir Tree* at Christmas.

- Gentle reminders were made about wastage and the children began to use the books more sensibly.

- The stories often mimicked the form of favourite published books in the classroom, and some were copied wholesale.

- Collaborative writing increased, with children working together on a story or a series based on an invented character.

- Children became more willing to try a spelling for themselves, and became less concerned about correctness at all times.

- Little books and stories began to arrive from home. Some parents complained about the amount of time the children spent writing stories at home!

Janet Karnacz, St. Paulinus R.C. Primary School, Guisborough, Cleveland

Extending the table

All teachers using a 'writing centre' or 'writing table' have found that the idea has evolved in the course of the year. In one school, the 'writing centre' became a 'question centre'. A post box was there to accept enquiries addressed to other children or members of staff.

Helen James from Hampshire summarises the focus on letter writing in her classroom.

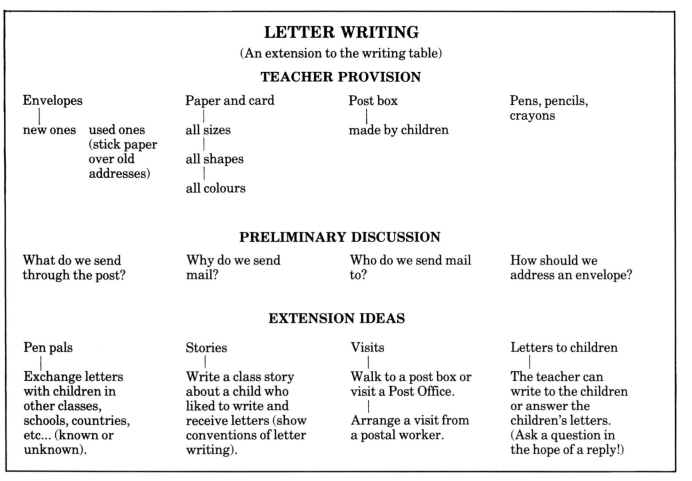

LETTER WRITING

(An extension to the writing table)

TEACHER PROVISION

Envelopes	Paper and card	Post box	Pens, pencils, crayons
new ones used ones (stick paper over old addresses)	all sizes all shapes all colours	made by children	

PRELIMINARY DISCUSSION

What do we send through the post?	Why do we send mail?	Who do we send mail to?	How should we address an envelope?

EXTENSION IDEAS

Pen pals	Stories	Visits	Letters to children
Exchange letters with children in other classes, schools, countries, etc... (known or unknown).	Write a class story about a child who liked to write and receive letters (show conventions of letter writing).	Walk to a post box or visit a Post Office. Arrange a visit from a postal worker.	The teacher can write to the children or answer the children's letters. (Ask a question in the hope of a reply!)

Teachers' comments

'Most of us in the Infant school felt that, initially, the provision of a writing area did lead to waste by the children, but that this was acceptable given the good and often surprising work that was produced. For established writing areas we felt that some input by the teacher would help to introduce new initiatives and increase motivation. For example, one could turn the writing area into a 'spell station' for spell-writing as part of a topic about witches. The Junior staff, too, sometimes felt the need for more teacher input, although they were trying to encourage more self-direction in their children.'

In making decisions about when and where writing should take place, teachers find that when children are engaged in purposeful activity there is a place for writing before, during and after the event. Steve Cummings found this when he took a group of his nursery children on an outing to Chinatown.

An opportunity to write

Attempting to encourage writing with a bilingual slant, we arranged a trip to Chinatown with a small group of nursery children. The idea was to have a day out, visit a Chinese restaurant and bring back props and food with which to set up our own restaurant in the nursery. We also took many photographs which were later used in a tape/slide presentation, with a commentary prepared by the children themselves. This was shown to all the children in the nursery and used as a classroom resource.

Back in the classroom, we provided menus, a variety of writing implements and books, including diaries, in which to write. Some Junior children decorated the windows of our restaurant using Chinese writing. Our hope was that the monolingual children's interest in other languages would be increased by coming into contact with written Chinese, and that the Chinese children would use their home language, both spoken and written, while taking part in role play in the 'restaurant'.

To a certain extent this happened. The Cantonese-speaking children spent proportionately more time in the restaurant than they had done in other types of role play, and they also used their home language more openly. We followed this up by cooking Chinese food, using authentic Chinese recipes. On one occasion a parent of one of the Chinese children gave a struggling teacher a welcome helping hand with a recipe. From the original idea of a Chinese restaurant, the idea of a Chinese school emerged. And so, with the help of some third and fourth year Juniors, a school was set up in the nursery.

The effect on the nursery children has been quite extraordinary. The sheer volume of bilingual writing that has emerged from the small beginnings of the Chinese restaurant three months ago has to be seen to be believed. This use of the first language did not appear only in the writing of the Chinese children. There were also examples of Tamil from a Tamil child, and monolingual English-speaking children were beginning to include Chinese-style writing in their work.

Nga, 4 years 9 months, writing in both Chinese and English

Steve Cummings, Grinling Gibbons School, ILEA

It is 10.00 a.m. The writing lesson begins. The topic is given, along with the writing book and a few helpful words.

The playtime bell means the end of the lesson; thirty minutes that seemed like an eternity to some and a brief time to others.

Under those conditions, writing is very much a hit and miss affair, the child having no time to think and plan ahead. Teachers and children need time to get involved in their writing so that even when they are away from the classroom, ideas and thoughts are being stored and shaped.

Beautiful but upside down

Some of the children entering the reception class had already done copy-writing at home. These children claimed that they could not write, and insisted that they dictate sentences to me and I scribe them. I complied with their wishes, observing that they then copied my writing beautifully but upside down. This reinforced my feeling that writing should be for reading and not for copying. My function, it seems to me, is to provide stimulus, support, encouragement and models of good adult writing, and to show the function and purpose of writing. I always indicate the importance of print when I am:

- reading stories and looking up information

- putting up notices

- writing letters and messages

- taking the register

- writing the children's names on drawers, pegs, book covers etc.

I use a variety of stimulus for writing:

- visits leading to posters or letters of thanks

- artefacts brought in for art and drama

- drama often involves writing: instructions for boat-building, spells for witches with short memories, advice and offers of help to Father Christmas, passports for journeys planned and letters home

Where are they going in their writing? I certainly know that they are growing into adults and that their writing grows and develops daily with them. Exactly how it develops in each individual I do not know. Their progression is obviously at an individual pace; what is a stimulus to one will have no effect on another. All I can do is to put as many clues as I possibly can in their way, and allow them to follow their own paths, picking up the clues in the order that is meaningful to them. Some are forging ahead, others are still at very early stages, but all are enjoying their writing and proud of sharing their achievements.

Jenny Brown, Somerset Bridge Primary School, Bridgwater, Somerset

Teachers sometimes feel threatened when the writing lesson no longer takes place at a set time each day. Here, a teacher describes how she sees her present role within her reception class.

Who is it for?

Writers need experience of writing in different ways, for different people. The more they write for others in a variety of contexts, the more proficient they will become at meeting the needs of their readers. The writing can also give them a sense of personal satisfaction. Because their writing is accepted, acknowledged and responded to, they continue to write, not just to communicate, but to give pleasure.

The teacher's role is a complex one here. (S)he needs to structure the opportunities so that children gain a broad experience of different uses of writing — from letters to biographies, from newspapers to instructions — and to ensure that these opportunities are supported by models of the written forms. At the same time, the responsibility for what is written, how and for whom needs to be given to the child so that the teacher's great idea isn't, in the child's mind, just another classroom chore.

The range of opportunities is great and includes:

- writing books, guides, notices and so on for younger children, for parents, for teachers
- sending and receiving invitations, letters, cards
- preparing and publishing magazines and newspapers for the school and community
- designing games for others to play

and many more.

Please can you tell us how you make the cakes?

How can we help young writers to understand the exigencies of a real audience? In the case of a reception class, the provision of a genuine audience will provide a focus for the children's writing, but it may also present them with a dilemma: they may be writing for an absent audience when their writing is still at a stage where they need to clarify it orally.

Should we resolve this dilemma by withholding real but absent audiences until later, or should we as adults scribe their voiced thoughts for them?

Perhaps this should not be regarded as an 'either/or' situation; maybe we need to consider ways of providing a real audience whose own need matches the skills of these emerging writers, and on other occasions to give children the opportunity of seeing their own words scribed by a more mature writer.

It was with these questions in mind that a writing liaison project was undertaken with a class of four- and five-year-olds in a Newcastle school.

Baking cakes became the catalyst for the writing, but at first we concentrated on shopping for the ingredients. Children visited the local supermarket armed with their 'lists' — sheets of card upon which labels identifying every ingredient were firmly stuck. The children matched the labels to those of goods on the shelves, and finally made their purchases.

The cakes were duly made, with plenty left over to send to children in the nursery class. Having dispatched the cakes with a signed card, the reception children eagerly awaited the response. Back it came in the form of a large 'thank you for the cakes' letter signed by the nursery children, with a request for the recipe so that they too could produce this gourmet feast. Excellent; the reception class had received a permanent record of the success of the cakes and the nursery now wanted the recipe. This, however, presented the reception class with a dilemma. They now had a real audience and a real purpose for writing, but how does one write a recipe for an audience of non-readers? They were discovering at first hand that the demands of a real audience can be quite taxing for a writer. The solution for this class lay within their own experience and, after lengthy deliberation, they set about constructing a recipe.

The children adapted their stuck-on shopping list method, and produced a sequenced recipe with packaging to show each ingredient — including the eggshells. Precise pictures of spoons showing quantities were carefully included within the 'method' part of the recipe. The finished pictogram recipe, with certain key words and phrases scribed by the teacher, stretched across the width of the

The following account is from a school where an opportunity to write purposefully and for a real audience arose quite naturally. It has much in common with many teachers' work throughout the country.

classroom. On completion, four children undertook the task of carefully delivering the recipe, winding their way through school corridors and halls until they reached the nursery.

The nursery audience 'read' the recipe and successfully baked their own cakes. Their only problem concerned the quantity of eggs required — was it three or six? It all depended on how you read the eggshells!

Through this collaborative venture both classes found a form of writing to each other that was suited to their own expertise and carefully tailored to suit the needs of their particular audience.

News of the recipe had by then spread throughout the school, and it presented an opportunity for the reception class to observe what happens if your audience changes and your writing has to accommodate a different range of writing experiences and expectations.

A number of eleven-year-olds were invited to borrow the cake recipe. They read, they cooked and they evaluated for themselves!

In answer to the question *'Was it easy to follow?'* the responses showed clearly that self-assessment provides children with opportunities for future learning: *'We measured the flour wrongly and put too much fat in. The first time they were very greasy. The second time they were nice.'*

This result seemed to highlight the different expectations of a more mature group of readers — perhaps they had skimmed the recipe too quickly or made hasty assumptions without 'reading the small print'.

The recipe was then re-written by the eleven-year-olds, for someone of their own age. The new versions were displayed with the original so that the reception class authors were provided with the opportunity to compare the contrasting styles, and recognise the importance of the needs of an audience.

Minnie Anderson, Tyneview Primary School, Newcastle

One important way to provide an audience for writing is through letter writing. Teachers have been very inventive in this area, as the following snapshots reflect.

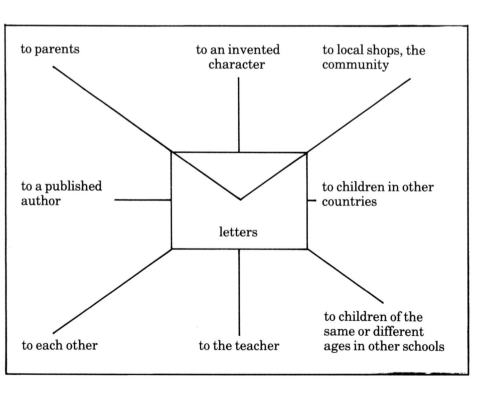

to parents

to an invented character

to local shops, the community

to a published author

to children in other countries

letters

to each other

to the teacher

to children of the same or different ages in other schools

One teacher set up a post box in the classroom to encourage the children to write freely. She suggested that the children could write to her or to each other. This form of letter writing proved to be a vehicle for the children to write about their own concerns.

Dear Mrs. Cooper

'Dear Paul, I'm suorry I have bene hordily to you now I'm going to be nice to you agin I want to know wuy you cicked my in the ridse, from Robert.'

'Dear Robert on incredible hulk dich you see the part whare his car had a puoncher in his wheel and he went mad and ternd green and poushed the car down a Hall and the puzzle in are class he Hazzant got his split shirt onit like He did on the film.'

'When I was making my shelter. I had a problem. theis is it you see. you know it is very difficult to stick twigs together with glue well I tried and tried and tried to think what to do then Robert was so helpful and give me long twigs for me to just cut hes a hero will anyway I had another problem because I had panted the wrong side well I had to glue that side again.'

Kath Cooper, St. John's First School, Frome, Somerset

Through writing letters to the author of one of their favourite books, the children in this account were able to use the information they had discovered for a real purpose, and to open a dialogue with a real writer.

Letters to an author

Seven-year-old children in a school in Devon investigated the life cycle of the butterfly as a Science project. The children kept caterpillars in the classroom and wrote logs of their progress, making daily observations over a half-term period. At the end of the study the teacher read them Eric Carle's *The Very Hungry Caterpillar.* The children discovered that their observations did not match Eric Carle's description. After a great deal of talk, discussion and brainstorming, the children and the teachers recorded the differences between the story text and their own observations.

Our caterpillars	The caterpillars in Eric Carle's story
	Blue caterpillar with green and yellow body
	Red face
	Shape of feet
	Orange feet
No antennae	Antennae on caterpillar
Long butterfly tongue curled up	Eyes too big
	No tongue
	Sun too big and sparkles
Eats only one sort of leaves	Caterpillars do not eat bits of anything or make nice round holes
Eats by nibbling edges sort of roundish	
Standing up on back legs when looking for food	
Walks in 'loops'	
Butterflies come out of cocoon and pump blood into the wings to make them stiff and blood drops on the floor in drips	No blood
	Eggs laid inside the apple
	Wings wrong shape and pattern

Although many of the children knew about the conventions of story writing and the licence of authors to write in the way they do, they still wanted to ask *'Have you ever observed caterpillars as we have done?'* It was decided to write a letter to Eric Carle to ask that question.

November 5th Thursday

Dear Eric Carle,
We like the book because it has got a hugry caterpillar in it You missed out some bits and we are going to tell you what you missed out the pumping blood part. before they are a butterfly and you must of obseved the caterpillar standing on his two back legs. Did you use you imagintion for lots of things? because I think you used your imagintion for lots of things. How could the caterpillar get throgh the lolipop when it is hard? I could not even bite a hard lolipop. And how could he or her get throgh the ice crem because it is to cold?

by
and
Donna
Julie
Donna
Julie
write back

The letter:

- reinforces their own knowledge
- enables that knowledge to be shared with their peers through the talk which preceded the writing
- allows them to reflect on their own experience
- questions someone else's experience
- provides a real purpose and audience for writing

Maisie Foster, Somerset Writing Project Co-ordinator, and Lynne Carre, Watcombe Primary School, Torbay, Devon

Children in the Project have been collaborating with each other to produce books and guides. Stories written by older children for younger ones have involved discussions about characters, storyline and presentation, as these letters show.

Books for children, by children

Thirteen-year-old Anwen writes to her four-year-old partner, Debbie:

Dear Debbie,

Thankyou for your letter and your picture. I am writing your book with lots of different things in it. I hope that I will be able to see you before I finish the book, so that we will be able to do some writing and drawing together for it.

love
from
Anwen
X

Suzanne negotiates the content of her story with her co-author:

Dear Joscelin,

dogs Are nice this is my care bers he is Pink. I like pink and yellow. I would like some rabbits in my book.

Love Suzanne ‡

In her evaluation of book writing for younger children,
Lisa, a twelve-year-old from Somerset, reflects:

Writing for the children was a really nice thing to do; you could tell they were excited about having the book by the letters they wrote to us

The most difficult thing was trying to produce a suitable story line which it was exciting & simple but was short and punchy and would keep their interest

I've learnt that writing for small children is a very very very hard and difficult thing to do

Further examples of children writing for different purposes and audiences can be found in the Theme Pack: *Audiences for Writing.*

All teachers stress the commitment shown by the children, not only to saying what they want to say, but also to writing and rewriting until the content and presentation satisfy the purpose and audience for which the writing was intended.

Teachers' comments

'Pupils were keen to work on these projects where their writing could be "shown off" and shared. Other teachers became involved (as in the Newcastle cookery example) and pupils certainly gained much pleasure from the letter exchange activities.'

Writing for other children and adults can be very rewarding, but there is also the need for children to experience writing for themselves. Such writing will range from personal reflections and recollections to more general speculations and the formulation of ideas.

When young children have been given their own books (variously referred to as 'learning logs', 'think books', 'journals'), some very interesting thoughts and questions have emerged.

Writing to themselves

In a Wiltshire school, at the beginning of a topic about the Victorians, one Infant wrote:

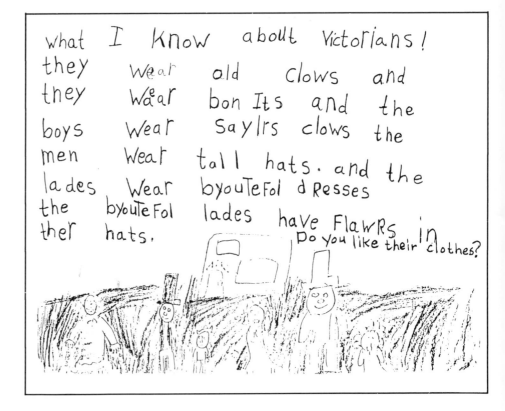

Another child speculated on what a Buddhist prayer drum might be like:

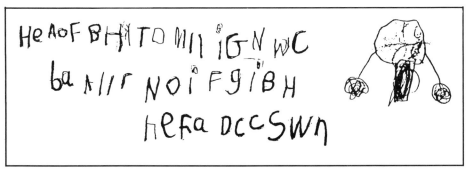

'I think it's sort of like a saucepan with a lid on, with some string and two balls. The balls hit it like a tennis ball. I could use it to make a tune.'

Sometimes the effort of thinking can produce an agonising response:

'I thought so much I couldn't build my bridge.'

There are further reflections on the use of writing for thinking in Section Three.

What do they do it with?

The resources given to young children to facilitate good writing have a profound influence on the final product. In the early planning stages, young children may need large sheets of paper on which to manoeuvre their thoughts. Once their initial ideas have developed, they will need access to many different types of paper and pens, and printing and reprographical resources.

These extracts from accounts of successful writing activities suggest how influential the writers' tools can be.

The first extract shows how the outcome of a writing activity may be influenced by the choice of paper and by the teacher's approach. This teacher was looking at the power of poetry to stimulate the children's imaginations and to encourage them to write fantasy.

Does the paper influence the writing?

I chose a selection of poems which contained evocative phrases but did not say explicitly what they were about. I read each poem three times, and then, as a class, we discussed what it seemed to be about. The discussions always became very lively.

I then proposed that the children could write a story about whatever the poem suggested to them. I explained that I would not be interfering in any way, and that I wanted them not to worry about spellings, and not to ask for help, but just to do their best. This procedure differed from that which the children were used to. They were given word books and dictionaries, writing paper and scrap paper for trying out spellings. Discussion continued in table groups throughout the writing process.

The first poem we used was 'The tuba' by Dawn Dejetes (aged 6).
The results were disappointing. The children were confused and distracted by having to work out their own spellings. Also, they had been given only one sheet of paper, and it seemed that once they had filled this, they did not want to write any more. I felt that in some way the single sheet had restricted them and I decided to find out whether the paper itself could become a visual aid to help them with their ideas.

For the next poem, 'Moon hops' by Ted Hughes, I made each child a small eight-page book from plain paper, and suggested that they could make story and picture books. We looked together at illustrated storybooks to see how they were compiled, and the children's enthusiasm and persistence increased noticeably. Some of the children started with a drawing, while some wrote first and then drew a picture on the facing page. The combination of pictures with writing seemed to help in moving from one stage in the story to the next.

The results were much better this time. All the stories were different; they were imaginative and humorous, and related to the poem very well. I was particularly interested to find that the spelling was, in fact, far better than I had expected.

Patricia Faulkes, James Watt Infant School, Birmingham

The next teacher worked with her class of five- and six-year-olds to write a book for younger children. This extract illustrates the central role of the materials.

In January 1987 we spent many sessions discussing the style and format of a variety of books. We found three different versions of *Little Red Riding Hood* and compared text and illustrations. We read books to ourselves, in pairs, in groups and as a class, involving ourselves in character and plot.

After a week I suggested we should each write a book to read and share with friends at a local First school. We discussed how our books could be presented, and the children favoured the idea of large colourful pictures accompanied by a supportive narrative.

I gave each child a piece of A4 paper, folded into eight sections, for a sequential plan of the main events of a story. The children worked out their ideas, drew rough sketches and wrote simple captions underneath. The sections were rather small but I felt this helped them to divide their stories and to structure their thoughts. This initial planning was carried out over a period of days. The children talked with their peers and with me, clarifying and developing their stories, adding more detail, and altering and amending original ideas.

When the children were ready, they began to copy into specially made books. I could sense a general feeling of discontent. The enthusiasm and sparkle were fading, although they continued without complaint. Was it too laborious for such young children to spend so much time on one piece of work? I looked closely at their books. Presentation and illustrations were being very carefully considered, but the effect was not striking. I gathered the children round and discussed this problem. The paper was of poor quality and the pencils they were using barely showed up. If they tried to rub out, the paper very quickly became discoloured or even wore away.

presented them with some white file paper of the type that the older children use. I drew a faint line two-thirds of the way down to separate the writing and the drawing. Two children then went to a fourth year class and asked if they could borrow one of their pens. I explained that great care would be needed if they used a pen, as no mistakes could be made. The results were so much better that everyone decided to use pen and file paper. The children were motivated by being treated like older children. They were very proud of their work and took great care with their handwriting and presentation.

There was only sugar paper or A4-sized card available in school, neither of which seemed suitable for making covers and pages. Gavin read his story to the head teacher and asked his advice on the best materials to make a book. As a result, thin A3 card in four colours was ordered. With help from some of the parents, the books were mounted, sewn and assembled. The children were thrilled to have become real authors, and showed their books with pride.

Vivienne Miller, Merley First School, Merley, Dorset

[A full version of this article is in the Theme Pack: *Audiences for Writing*.]

Technological tools

Computers exploded into schools in the early nineteen-eighties in a blaze of national publicity. Teachers suddenly realised that they didn't quite know what they were going to do with them. Mistakes were made and at first it seemed to many that the machine was dictating to them and they were losing control. Fortunately, though, new programs and facilities have more recently introduced into the learning process a control that was often missing. Hardware like the 'Concept Keyboard' and word processing packages such as 'Pendown' and 'Writer' have offered opportunities to release young writers from the mechanics of writing. Computers and word processors are now being seen both as a stimulus for writing and as a way to aid the process. However, as with all tools for learning, the enabling role of the teacher takes on a heavy significance. The machine won't teach the children to write, and appropriate intervention by the teacher is needed more than ever.

The computer can improve the content of the writing of even very young children. It can have a significant influence on their attitude to the process of writing, especially towards editing and revising their work. The pencil is not thrown away, but is used alongside the computer. Each draft print-out is revised and reworked, but the children don't have to copy out their new drafts again and again. Furthermore, the poorest pencil manipulator can have the pleasure of a very professional-looking final product.

I have been looking at the role the computer has played in facilitating writing both in my own classroom and in other schools in Somerset and Wiltshire. In doing so, I have been particularly concerned with:

- motivation
- composition and transcription
- editing and revising

Motivation

The majority of children take to using a computer for writing with a readiness that is often surprising. However, their initial reasons for being enthusiastic are probably not to do with a realisation that the computer could help improve the *content* of

This account illustrates how a word processor can be used as a very dynamic tool.

their writing. The main responses I have had to the question, *'Why do you like using this word processor for your writing?'* have been to do with the surface features of the writing, especially the tidiness of the presentation.

I first noticed this in my own class of eleven-year-olds, but I have recently heard the same response from six-year-olds who had been using a word processor for a short while.

> I like useing the coputer because it has got a delete presser if you use pencil and you RVb it out it is dirty.

Even in a child who had been taught that it is the *ideas* which are important in the initial draft, and that spelling and presentation come at a later stage, the response was still one of wonder at the ease with which mistakes could be completely eradicated.

Children enjoy the novelty of the computer: coping with the unfamiliar order of the keyboard, discovering that the auto-repeat on the key means that you merely peck the keys or else you get a string of letters, and at the same time writing a piece of work about that morning's assembly.

However, during one session I observed the constraints put upon them by this very different way of writing. I could see, from the work that they did with a pencil and paper, that the unfamiliar letter order on the keyboard and the need to remember spaces between words slowed down their production a great deal at first. After about twenty minutes, though, they had all mastered the more obvious features and were speeding up considerably.

Towards the end of the session they needed the word *'exercise'*, but were unsure as to its spelling. I happened to know that it was in the dictionary that was part of the word processing system we were using. I showed them how to find the word, and consequently it appeared, as if by magic, in the text. Later, they needed the word *'exciting'*, and proceeded to find it themselves without any aid from me. It was obvious from the talk going on at the time that they derived a great deal of satisfaction from the degree of autonomy they had in performing this task. When, later, they wrote about using the computer, the dictionary facility was mentioned frequently.

Composition and transcription

In schools we almost invariably ask our children to be author and secretary rolled into one; we then sometimes compound our felony by asking them to complete the writing task in one shot. The models we give them for written work — often published works — are usually lavish, word-perfect productions. My own class were amazed to see a copy of a Roald Dahl manuscript with all the corrections and insertions made by the author. Some of them had assumed that he wrote his books in one go, and sent them off to be printed. By showing children that writing is something which progresses through several stages before becoming the finished publication, we can help them to develop their own skills as writers in a more structured way. In using the word processor with my children, I have been able to observe the relative ease with which they come to terms with the problems they have as writers when they are allowed to cope with one new skill at a time.

Editing and revising

Manipulation of text is much easier when a word processor is used. Children can concentrate their energies on editing and revising specific parts of what they have written, rather than dissipating them in the process of rewriting the whole.

When I first started to use word processors with the children, I found it easy to explain the idea of editing a piece of work at the appropriate time. I found it much more difficult to make them look critically at their work; to see if what they had written actually said what they meant it to say and, if it didn't, to reshape their text so that it did. I tried to encourage children to share their work with a trusted response partner who would be able to make constructive comments.

Employing this strategy with children has been a slow process. Many of them are of the opinion that what they have sweated to produce shall not lightly be changed and, if we are to accept the argument that the children need to be in control of their writing, to force change upon them is counter-productive.

The use of word processors in conjunction with the use of response partners has made revision of text easier to achieve. When the children are writing at the computer they constantly read through what is displayed before them on the screen. If a response partner is there too, interaction can take place as the work is in progress, points being discussed as they are fresh in the writer's mind. Moreover, the computer's capacity to provide multiple print-outs of a piece of written work means that several people can read the same piece at once, facilitating group discussion.

Bill Urwin, Broadway Neroche County Primary School, Ilminster, Somerset

The micro classroom

At Inmans Primary School, the micro has become an integral part of school life. It is situated near the centre of a large open-plan area.

The Humberside Project looked specifically at the use of the micro in the classroom.

The six- and seven-year-old children have now been using the micro for writing for approximately two terms, working initially in groups. The teacher has become aware of the value of collaborative writing, and has found ways of integrating it with individual writing. The children begin their topic work by discussing the theme in groups, which helps them to raise ideas and to organise their thoughts. They then work individually on a piece of writing, either using the micro or on paper.

It is noticeable that children using the micro constantly read through their writing, editing and also reorganising their thoughts as they work. They are evidently willing to experiment and take risks with their work, in the knowledge and security that if an idea doesn't work it can be quickly deleted.

Once the first draft is finished, a copy is printed for the child. This copy is taken back to the group where it is read to the other children and discussed. This conferencing is very important; the other children raise questions and make suggestions about the content of the writing. The child then returns to the micro to redraft and edit the text as appropriate.

Using this very simple method of working, the teacher (with the aid of the micro) is helping the children to develop an understanding of the drafting/editing process. Although each child is producing an individual piece of work, the children also have the advantage of collaboration along the way. This provides an audience and feedback for the writing.

The teacher has also noticed that she no longer has to worry about motivating the children to write, and that even the reluctant writers are keen to commit their ideas to the micro. The children are also writing with increased motivation when using pencil and paper.

Sylvia Emerson, David Bowen and John Hurst, Humberside Writing Project

(Further discussion of micros in the classroom can be found in the Theme Pack: *Writing and Micros*.)

How do they do it?

Writing is a complex set of practices which is far more than a set of skills. We have all experienced what it means to be a writer: the difficulties of generating ideas; the decisions about how to express yourself effectively; the displacement activities like making another cup of tea; the concerns about whether you've hit the right tone and achieved the right effects; the physical tiredness and, sometimes, the satisfaction.

Of course, the difficulties vary according to the task. If you're writing a shopping list you'll worry more about the ideas than the presentation; if filling in a form, presentation may be more important. In many tasks in school it is the initial planning, the ideas stage, that is problematic.

Manchester teachers who were asked to write during a Project meeting described some of their feelings as writers.

I can quite honestly say that when I was asked to write I felt sick, and the thoughts of childhood flooded back. Panic is the feeling I had when asked to write at our first meeting — it was the thought of having to share the writing, the results, with other adults. Once I was assured that this was not going to happen, I enjoyed the opportunity to write for myself, and am now much more aware of the process we go through as writers.

- A feeling of panic . . .
- What would I write?
- What could I write?
- What will people think of my efforts?
- Will it be worth anything?
- Panic subsided somewhat when we were told we did not have to put our name on the piece.

- What do I put down?
- How will it be received and judged?
- Will I be expected to read it out loud?
- Thought about not having enough time to complete.
- Lost 'flow' of thoughts when couldn't find the right word. Lost the rhythm.

Children can give interesting oral accounts of events, but when it comes to writing down the ideas, they often get lost in the minefield of transcription. They need help in sorting their ideas. The next article demonstrates how such sorting can take place.

A framework for writing

'News' forms a staple part of the curriculum in many Infant classrooms. It has been described as the seedbed from which expressive writing develops, yet in practice much of it seems stereotyped and 'done to order'. Our aim was to discover what children themselves consider newsworthy and, by using their ideas, to explore how this kind of writing might be developed.

By inviting a class of six- and seven-year-olds to list their suggestions for news, we were able to identify a 'top fourteen'. Family and friends featured substantially ('My Mum', 'My Nan', 'My friend', 'My family', 'My brother'), together with the pets, possessions and places that make up the home environment ('My books', 'My toys',

'My room', 'My dog', 'My house', 'My car'). There was only one example of a special outing ('A visit to the Zoo') and only one rather indirect mention of school ('On the way to school').

An earlier examination of news-writing throughout the school had shown that young children often find it difficult to keep to a subject. As they come under increasing pressure to write more, they tend to accumulate several events rather than to develop one. Seven-year-old Michael's news is typical of the kind of chronological catalogue that results:

'On Saturday my cousin came to sleep with me and on Sunday we went to Park Parade and the next day he sleeped again and in the morning we went out to play up the park and we went on the swings and then we went on the climbing frame to play up for touch.'

We wanted to see how children might be helped to focus their attention more sharply, and elaborate on specific ideas.

Each session began with a class discussion. In the early sessions, a teacher-selected topic from the 'top fourteen' was written on a large sheet of paper, the children were asked to suggest things to say about it and their ideas were written down by the teacher. As soon as the teacher began to write, the quality of talk changed. The children began to formulate and dictate their ideas as captions.

We wanted the children to see how ideas can be put together to make a text. Once their contributions had been written down, we showed them how some ideas overlapped or were related and could therefore be grouped together. The material on 'My Mum', for instance, fell into two main categories — 'What she looks like' and 'What she does for me'. These headings were written on to another, larger, sheet of paper and, as the teacher helped the children decide which of their initial statements belonged to each category, a second adult wrote a new, re-ordered draft. This allowed us not only to demonstrate the writing process, but also to introduce terminology which describes that process and which enables children to think objectively about it.

The class text then served as a model for the children's own writing on the same topic. Perhaps inevitably, most of them stayed very close to what had already been written and produced pieces that had the kind of flatness we had hoped to avoid. We needed to think more carefully about producing a framework for writing which would encourage spontaneity instead of acting as a straitjacket.

We soon came to realise that the ordering of ideas could be fostered through the ordering of talk. Initially we had encouraged brainstorming, with ideas coming together in a fairly random way, but in later sessions we asked the children to sustain and develop what they were saying before moving on to something else. As a result, the children learned to organise their ideas in speech before they did so in writing. Instead of recording all the details of the discussion, we now wrote down only the main headings which then became the plan to which the children wrote.

Talk allowed individual children to make their meanings more explicit. Both the content and the linguistic complexity of Ralph's *'My mum loves me'* were extended when, by means of a question, he was encouraged to add *'because she is always kissing me'*. This then served as a model for other speakers and writers who began to use the same syntactic pattern.

We worked from the premise that writing needs to be shared. One form of sharing is to involve everyone in the classroom in the activity of writing, adults and children alike. In writing alongside the children we not only made a positive statement about the nature and importance of writing, we also discovered for ourselves how hard the generation of news can be, since everyday life tends to be routine and uneventful.

Children and adults also shared their writing by reading it aloud, not at the end of the session, but while it was in progress. By talking about what had been written, we were able to focus the children's attention on the possibilities of the subject as well as to develop a sense of audience.

By the final session, both we and the children were familiar with our way of working and the topic 'My best friend', selected by the teacher from the 'top fourteen', gave great scope for personal response.

My best Friend has short Hair
and he is a Good fighter
he is the best fighter in the school
and we race in the Playground
and he looks after me

Michael

Margaret Axford, King Alfred's College, Winchester, and Roger Mulley, Hampshire Writing Project Co-ordinator

'Boo Hoo' and other stories

Following the reading of stories featuring sequences of animals (including 'Boo Hoo' and 'Poor old Polly' from the *Story Chest* series), the children had great fun making up similar rhymes. So we agreed to write, all starting off with the same sentences but then working individually. Sami's story actually goes round in a circle:

Old Polly bought a dolly she swapped
It for a LoLy The LoLy was too slopy
saw she swapped it for a Pigly The pigly was
too big saw she swapped it
for a dgr (digger) The digr wudnt
wock. saw she swapped
it for a wam (worm) The
wam wsa too
croly saw
she swapped
it for a
dolly

> No writer of any age can manage to create texts without the support of writing models. One major source of such models in the early years is books, that rich resource of stories, poems and nursery rhymes. In these examples from the Cleveland Project, teachers demonstrate the structural support for writing provided by published texts.

Whilst reciting 'This little pig went to market', I asked what the little pig might have needed at the market. This led to a book called 'The five little pigs'. However, no one wanted to write about the pig who had none, so the children said I would have to do it.

This little pig went to market

He hadno food to eat

This little pig stayed at home
Becos He had the chikn Pocz He fech
a Kofy then He went Bac too bed
He Red a BUK and He went
too Sliip then   sum bdy
noct on the dor

This little pig had roast beef

cos he   wos ungry so
he Atit sum roast beef so so
         tol upso he did

This little pig had none

because he wantec
fish fingers and
there weren't any
in the fridge.

This little pig said "Wee wee
wee" all the way home
cos He fell ovre
on   the gravl
cos a
tast   fox Had
on   Him and He fel ovr
     the
         gravl

Books such as *The Jolly Postman* (A & J Ahlberg), *Dear Zoo* (Rod Campbell), *Brown Bear, Brown Bear* (Eric Carle) and *The Shopping Basket* (John Burningham) have stimulated innovative and humorous responses. Two illustrations will have to suffice.

I wet toThe zoo
ahd ISO a shak
Itc hembac
bothe was toscery

*I went to the zoo
and I saw a snake
I took him back but
he was too scary*

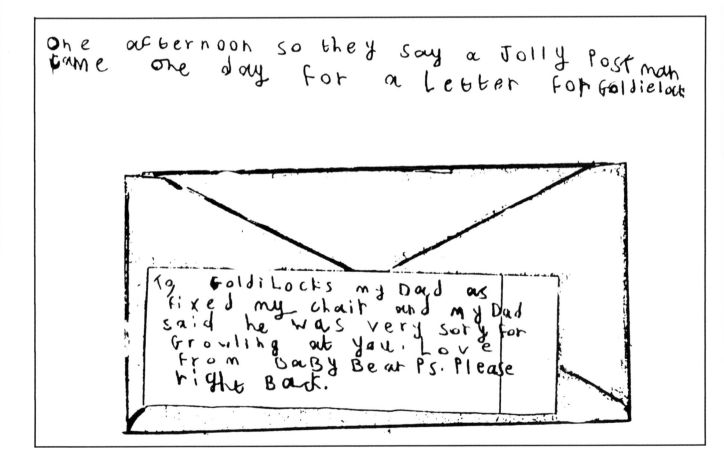

One afternoon so they say a Jolly Postman came one day for a Letter For Goldielock

To GoldiLocks my Dad as fixed my chair and my Dad said he was very sorry for Growling at you. Love from BaBy Bear Ps. Please right Back.

Drawing on experience

One way of helping children to express in writing what they can easily express orally, is to use the medium of drawing. Adapted into particular patterns, pictures can become strategies for planning, a way of brainstorming ideas and then selecting and organising them. It means that even very young children are able to communicate their experiences in an exciting way. The drawings become a rehearsal for their writing. Even at the top end of the First school, the technique of planning through drawing can release children from the constraints of transcription, enabling them to concentrate on organising their ideas.

We had two starting points. First, we wanted to find a way in which children might be helped to shape an experience into a clearly defined anecdote and secondly, we wanted them to plan their stories as a whole so that they could see the overall structure for themselves.

We found a clue to the way experience might be shaped in Andrew Wilkinson's phrase 'the disruption of probability'. Good stories often involve the unexpected, when the normal pattern of events is abruptly disturbed. Many books for children exploit this narrative device, and we began to collect published stories which might provide good working models for the children's own writing. These included Jill Murphy's *On the Way Home,* John Prater's *On Friday Something Funny Happened* and the Ahlbergs' *Fred's Dream.*

A second clue was provided by a child who regularly drew sequences of pictures to record her own stories, an approach that enabled her quite literally to see the story sequence in its entirety.

We began with Jill Murphy's *On the Way Home.* The story was already a firm favourite with our class of five- to six-year-olds and, since they were always having minor accidents, it was a theme they could readily make their own. Within small groups we shared the story, recalled our own experiences and then began to record them: first in a picture sequence, next in oral storytelling and only finally in writing. To help the children shape the event we focused on three main stages: what the child was doing just before the accident, the accident itself (or disruption of probability) and what happened next.

The combination of a narrative focus and the opportunity to rehearse the story, first in pictures, then in talk, seemed to help the children structure their experience more effectively.

The quality of work that was produced encouraged us to try out the same idea across a wider age range. We also experimented with different narrative themes, to see if some were better suited to a sequencing approach than others, and with different kinds of format to see if pictorial layout had any significant effect on the way the writing was subsequently organised.

We discovered that picture sequencing worked well right across the five- to ten-year-old age range. Many of the older children enjoyed and benefited from the opportunity to realise their stories in pictorial form before they moved on to writing. Even those who had become self-conscious about their lack of artistic skill were ready to use the technique, once they realised that the pictures were intended to sketch out the story and need not be regarded as a finished product. We suspect that drawing becomes secondary to writing far too early for many children, and we would like to see opportunities for picture planning throughout the Primary school and possibly beyond.

Creating time for talk between the drawing stage and the writing stage had positive effects across the age range. Although the quality of the younger children's oral storytelling was generally higher than that of their writing, the spoken rehearsal clearly reinforced the children's ordering of events and helped each to find a voice.

We also noticed that at the age of about eight, children began to incorporate words into their pictures. This was usually done if the drawing alone was incapable of

From the work described in an earlier article, Margaret Axford and Roger Mulley went on to look at picture planning.

53

conveying the full meaning, but some of the children began to recognise the potential of this technique for focusing on critical detail and recording words and phrases that might be useful to them once they began to write. We had previously observed that young children sometimes find brainstorming difficult. They tend to write text from the outset, recording complete captions rather than noting down single words. However, this new development suggests that a combination of words and pictures might provide an effective introduction to the brainstorming technique, allowing children to capture in words the ideas they cannot draw and to record in pictures those they cannot write.

this is me and my Mam and my cousins they came to school with us

This is Mr melley saying the register

This is geting Ready to go on the trip

This is us going through the Park

This is us in the stream

This is us climbed the stile

and this is us going back to the school

Theresa

Clearly the strategies we have described have much potential for helping young children to organise their stories, but the appropriateness of the format to the task needs to be considered carefully. The children's accounts of their visit to the stream (see example above) made us realise that a linear sequence may be a drawback if there is no clear 'disruption of the probable' to shape events, since it merely reinforces the tendency to catalogue what happened. This led us to explore different kinds of layout which might be used more effectively for such events. An autumn walk was recorded in a four square pattern, with each square dedicated to a different sense — hearing, smell, sight and touch. Not all the sensations could be drawn, so the children used a blend of words and pictures to note down their experiences. By emphasising theme rather than narrative, this planning device helped them to focus on significant aspects of their walk instead of attempting to catalogue the whole in a chronological way. It also influenced the form in which they subsequently wrote, as the material lent itself more readily to a poetic form than to a narrative one.

Children may need guidance on how many pictures to use for their story. A blank sheet of paper with no parameters is too open a task for them to cope with. On the other hand, structure needs to be balanced by flexibility if the children's ideas are to be adequately accommodated. We also need to be more flexible about when the children write. Initially we expected them to produce their stories in one sitting. More recently we have discovered that the writing can usefully be sustained over an extended period of time. Once the story has been sketched out in its entirety, it is possible for older children to write it one section at a time, without losing their impetus or sense of direction. This also allows for more talk at each stage of the story, so that attention is focused not only on structure but also on incidental detail.

As we used this planning technique across the age range we found that some of the older children were showing a preference for words over pictures. This was a salutary reminder that, however successful picture planning might be, no one approach is suited to all children in all circumstances. We need to give them a range of techniques for organising their experience so that ultimately they are able to choose the one best suited to the task and to their own preferred ways of working.

Margaret Axford, King Alfred's College, Winchester,
and Roger Mulley, Hampshire Writing Project Co-ordinator

Teachers' comments

'Very positive and enthusiastic responses from all pupils involved. Some — especially older children who were given a rare opportunity to think through drawing — spent very long periods of time on this work and were very keen to continue.'

Does drafting help?

When drafting, children learn that writing is not a one-off event. Initially, ideas are more important than presentation. Drafting involves jotting down ideas, sentences, even sequences, possible spellings of words to be used; this can take place with or without the aid of the teacher, alone, with a partner, or in groups. I have found that seven-year-old reluctant writers respond favourably to the technique. Experimenting with drafting focused my own attention on the process of writing and the problems and anxieties which children face.

Worries about spelling

First, we had to find a method of reducing the children's fear of mis-spelling a word. We had to encourage them to give priority to ideas rather than spellings. It was suggested to them that they try to spell all the words themselves, but if they were uncertain about spelling a word, they were to draw a ring around it.

The teacher as a model

The idea of drafting was introduced when the children were writing their news. I did my own drafting on the board, setting out the events of the weekend in chronological order, for example: *'washing machine broke down, did shopping, visited a friend'*. I then proceeded to redraft the notes.

The conference

One of the most crucial aspects of the success of drafting seemed to be the conference that happens after drafting. This gave the child and the teacher an opportunity to extend the ideas or unravel the confusion before (and not after) the final presentation.

I found that older children could continue with a piece of work which had been set aside, and so continuity of writing activity has been improved. The children can now read through their draft notes in their folders, formulate their own ideas, and so increase their independence. Work is no longer seen as a one-off activity which must be finished in one session. The children have become aware of the *process* of writing rather than just the product, and less anxiety is experienced about producing the final piece of work.

Liz Gale, Oakwood County First School, Hampshire

Another important aspect of the writing process is drafting. Children often have the belief that once something has been written down it cannot be changed. It may be that they have never seen a mature writer at work, and noted what an untidy business it can be. Supporting writing development can come in many forms, as this account of work in a Hampshire school demonstrates.

Draft drawing

Artists have been showing us the way — drafting their work and displaying their drafts as part of the development of a work of art. At a recent exhibition of Picasso's sketchbooks, I was delighted to see his drafts of a major work with the stages of development clearly shown. What a celebration of process.

As a language support teacher, I have observed children's concern for perfection

In this account, young children are introduced to the planning and drafting processes through drawing.

and neatness from their earliest years in school. It is not clear whether this concern is because of a fear of being wrong, acquired at an early age, or because they personally enjoy the neatness of their presentation. Some children are afraid to write in case they make a mistake. They continually look for teacher approval, and some consequently reject writing as being all too difficult. Many hang like limpets on to their rubbers and word books and won't write without them. They want to check every spelling before writing a word.

I wanted to devise a strategy that would encourage beginning writers to look for change in their work, encourage risk-taking, and encourage the children to enjoy their writing. Because children were so intent on making their drawings 'right', I decided to encourage them with draft drawing. I wanted to introduce the language to them: 'drafting'; 'cutting and sticking'; 'conferencing'. I wanted them to see that their drawings could be discussed and altered, and be part of a creative process. I wanted them to be able to tell their own story, and to be proud of their final product.

The process used with four-year-old children

We sat in a circle and I read the children a story, *Ben's Box* — a pop-up book illustrated by Michael Foreman. It is about the imaginative journeys of a little boy and his cat with the empty box in which his mother's washing machine had just arrived. Ben has a series of adventures: he fights dragons near a castle; he is involved in a shipwreck; he travels underwater and through space; he flies in the sky.

After reading the story I asked the children to close their eyes, and picture the box and a place to which they would like to go in it. I then asked the children to share the places to which they had 'travelled in their heads'.

The children observed me writing down the information, and then I gave them a sheet of A4 sugar paper. I asked them to draw the place — just the place. In no time the backgrounds were drawn and coloured in. I then gave each of them smaller sheets and asked them to draw a picture of themselves in this place. Some discovered that they had problems with scale, and they drew different versions until they were satisfied with the result. As they moved their small drawings around the background sheet, the stories changed and developed. Some asked for larger sheets of paper, so that their picture could grow. Whenever they wished to remember more details of their journey, they closed their eyes, and 'saw' their pictures again.

It was now time to cut and stick. In a separate area of the room, the children laboriously cut out their figures, clouds, spaceships etc, and stuck them on to the background, some telling their story as they worked, some arguing with themselves... Each child worked independently. Some asked for paper and wrote; I acted as scribe for others.

Finally we sat down again in our circle, and shared the stories the pictures told.

In this way, the children were introduced at the beginning of their school life to:

Visualising images they wished to draw/write about, and creating their own stories.

Conferencing — they were encouraged to share, to listen, to discuss and to encourage each other in their work.

Drafting — reshaping their stories visually helped children to reshape them verbally. Changing their work — re-drawing it — became part of the process of creating.

The work was later displayed in a part of the room called the 'Magic Box'. There, the children continue to 'travel'. Every now and again the theme is changed: under the sea; on the moon; in Iceland.

I have always taken the children through the various stages of the strategy in one long session. It has been a source of amazement to me that such small children are able to concentrate and work for such a long stretch of time — yet another educational theory disproved. The strategy usually takes all morning (with the children taking an unwilling playtime break) — perhaps too long for a class teacher to spend with demands from other children to be taken into consideration. The different activities involved can, though, be spread over a number of days. Moreover, the draft drawing need not be individually done; highly successful collaborative pictures and stories can be created by small groups.

Carole Mason, Somerset Writing Project Co-ordinator

Providing support

Six-year-old Fiona is a fluent talker with a wide vocabulary, but, until very recently, she had achieved neither quality nor quantity in her writing. She had begun using *Breakthrough* in the reception class, and during the following year she continued to offer only one or two short, scrappy sentences, reluctantly written. Because she was obviously capable of doing more, I took what appeared to be the next logical step and gave her a *Breakthrough* Word Book. This had the effect of slowing down the flow of her writing even more, and the Word Book was withdrawn.

The next stage was initiated by Fiona herself. She began asking me to write words for her, and copying them straight into her book. She didn't construct the whole sentence first in her green holder, as in normal *Breakthrough* practice. I allowed this to pass without comment, and waited to see what would develop. I found the next stage astonishing. Fiona produced a whole page of writing in an easy, flowing style, although there were many spelling mistakes. She had made no reference to teacher, Word Book or Sentence Maker, and wrote much more rapidly and attentively than ever before.

Despite the inaccuracies, many common words were in fact spelled correctly from memory, and invented spellings such as *'chram' (tram), 'jrunck' (drunk), 'lunt' (learned), 'ckum' (come)* reflected a brave and confident attempt to use the phonic understanding she had developed so far.

I now consider that, because of my liking for the structure of the *Breakthrough* system, I had tried to channel Fiona's writing through stages which may not have been appropriate for her. Clearly, she had found such disciplines restrictive, and it seems likely that her present standard of fluent and enthusiastic writing could have been reached much earlier without them. Obviously, she will need support and experience to improve spelling and presentation, but Fiona now clearly considers herself to be a writer, and uses writing to express herself.

I feel that Fiona's experience needs to be borne in mind where others are concerned. It seems to support the theory that children should be given choice from a range of approaches to writing, and that teachers need to experiment, observe and adapt the support they offer according to the ways in which different children respond.

Joan Dunbavin, James Watt Infant School, Birmingham

> **Through experience, we develop preferences for particular ways of supporting writing development. No system, though, is likely to be appropriate for every child and every class. Here, an Infant teacher considers the use of *Breakthrough to Literacy* (Longman) as a method of supporting a particular child.**

Who owns the writing?

Children need to have control of their own learning. Teachers in the National Writing Project have realised that children have a wealth of knowledge about writing and about their world. This is frequently mentioned in discussions about child-centred education but perhaps, in everyday practice, there are restrictions on children's responsibility for what is discussed and for how material is expressed in writing.

Infant teachers understand the importance of encouraging children to think and question in active learning situations. Children build upon what they already know, using their own language and images to help them understand.

> **A Wiltshire teacher explored a range of strategies for helping children to think through their writing.**

Two concerns made me look at 'think writing', using 'think books', for Infants:

1 Some children were quite willing to let other children do their thinking and talking for them. There were always extroverts who dominated group discussions. I wanted to know what each child was thinking before his or her thoughts had been influenced by group conversation.

2 Current research emphasises that writing should be used as a tool for learning: writing to learn, to discover connections, to describe processes, to express emerging understandings, to raise questions and to find answers. I wanted to encourage such writing for learning.

The work in the classroom before the introduction of the 'think books' is very important. There needs to be discussion based on questions such as *What is thinking?* and *How do we think?* A good open-ended question at this point is, *Which is better at thinking: a brain or a computer?*

---

my body

my body can consontrat we consont

BY usping your Brain To Think like I am now. the Brain is in your head and you store all the Things you now in there untill you need it. my baly can walk. I walk by moveing my legs and toes my musals and knees. I Bend my knees poush up and down or my toes and stand on my masol.

I like to give Infants a book for their 'think writing' because it gives their thoughts a status and provides a permanent record. They need to understand, though, that their first priority is to get their thoughts on paper, without breaking off to ask for spellings. The children need to feel secure at this stage with their own emergent writing.

Jo Stone, Wiltshire Writing Project Co-ordinator

In this account, five-year-olds responded very positively to their own 'think books'.

As part of the Writing Project, 'think books' were introduced to my middle Infant class as a private journal or personal diary. They would write in the books by themselves, only when they wished to do so. They could consider writing about personal feelings as well as events — as in the 'news books' children used to write.

Initially the children were hesitant, and some were disturbed by the request to write something down unaided. Typical responses were: *I can't do it!* and *How do you write (x)?*

At that point I felt concerned that the children were being asked to do something beyond their capabilities, so we left the 'think books' for a week. Then the idea took off quite spontaneously. Janine announced that she had something to write, and produced the following:

The photographer took my photograph on the stage, there was a bear

Joseph's ingenuity showed up in the following piece of writing:

It's interesting to note the strategies the children employ in constructing words for themselves. Their unconventional spelling is often remarkable, as in Janine's writing *'vtografae'* for *photographer.* How clever for a five-year-old! The children continue to teach me every day.

Jean Miller, St. Michael's Infant School, Newcastle

What happens to it?

The emphasis in all the accounts reported above has been on the writing task having a real purpose and a real audience. Texts are created not simply for the teacher to assess writing development, but because particular messages are to be conveyed to specific people — recipes for the nursery children, books for younger children, letters to authors and so on.

Such writing is going to receive a response from different sources and at different points in its production: from peers, from the teacher and from the intended audience. Teacher response at the beginning may well be concerned with developing the ideas rather than spelling or punctuation:

HOOS BEENSITINGMAK CHER
SEDBEBB BER ANDBROWKit
who did it kendal ? I know, do you ?

GOWLDLOSe

Response may come from critical readers other than the teacher, such as a published author. For example, the drafts of a story written as a result of a visit from writer June Counsel were sent to her for comment:

This is a lovely little story. Although it is so short, it has everything in it. Fear, running away, sadness, then help, and help from an unexpected character, a friendly dog, and, finally a safe happy ending and a reward for the good dog. It is satisfying as it stands but if you were to re-write it, you might like to bring the two girls in and let them explain that they weren't going to hurt James, perhaps say what they were doing in the forest.

June Counsel

[A full report of this exchange and further examples of ways of responding to writing can be found in the Theme Pack: *Responding to and Assessing Writing*.]

Who else is involved?

The child's 'community of writers' extends far beyond the classroom, and recognition needs to be made of the kinds of writing and writers available to children.

The Pond Project

Although there was no problem in getting parents to do the physical work, they were initially non-committal in their response to the request to write about it! The idea of coming in to school to write obviously worried them greatly. They were, therefore, given the choice: to write in school with their child, or, if they preferred, to write at home with their child about their shared experience.

Having managed to persuade the parents to do some writing, the staff were delighted with the change in their perception of the writing tasks undertaken by children every day in school. They became aware of, and eager to discuss with the teacher, the process of writing. They began to look at content rather than at presentation. They became alive to the importance of real purposes and audiences for children's writing, and began to comment on how such strategies led to more meaningful and more enthusiastic writing.

Once the initial barriers were broken down, the teachers found that the children were bringing into school pieces of writing that they and their parents had worked on together, often with the children illustrating and the parents scribing.

An activity aiming to involve parents in the writing process occurred in Cleveland when Normanby Primary School engaged in a Pond Project. Parents were asked to help dig a pond, a shared activity which led to much planning, thinking, observing and, of course, writing, by parents as well as children. Following the activity, the teachers reflected on the project.

61

During the following two terms, the school began to look closely at the benefits of parental involvement in children's writing. These benefits were most obvious in terms of an increased enthusiasm in the children's approach to the writing task. Hand-made books were taken home, and completed stories, written by parents and children, were returned with pride. On their own initiative, some parents and children began keeping holiday journals, and this idea quickly spread. Parents talked to staff about their new appreciation of the effort and concentration that children employ when writing, and about how writing with their children had helped them reach this understanding. Staff quickly became aware that the profile of writing in school had been raised enormously by parental involvement. Parents began to ask children, *'What have you written today?'*

```
May I say, I also enjoyed

making new friends as well as

meeting all the children's teachers.


It was a most pleasant


experience.

                    Yours gratefully,

          Mr. Paul Munroe.
```

There was some spin-off across all the age groups in the school. Children in the nursery became involved and some writing was done with parents; some children began writing collaboratively; older children scribed for younger ones who wished to have articles included in the Upper school magazine; books were written; letters to various agencies were written by children and replies were received; letter and book exchanges were established with another school.

What was the secret of getting parents involved in this way? It was obviously necessary to make them feel welcome and valued. It was important that staff should take time to explain to them, perhaps over a cup of tea or coffee, exactly what would be required when they were taken into the classroom; there is little time to talk things through with the demands of thirty children waiting to be met. Parents often feel that education has changed so much since they were at school that they might do the wrong thing. Time taken to explain what is happening (and why) pays off enormously in terms of parents' confidence in the classroom, their usefulness to children and staff, and their willingness to come back again.

Normanby Primary School, Cleveland

[Many more examples of involving other people in children's writing are to be found in the Theme Pack: *Writing Partnerships 1: home, school and community.*]

Shared writing — a support strategy

In the very early years, children usually write collaboratively with the teacher so that the result is not always limited by the children's physical writing abilities.

The strategy of shared writing has been explored in detail by Manchester teachers working mainly in nursery and reception classes. Their findings are summarised here.

Shared writing is

- working with children to help them construct their stories by acting as scribe
- making teaching points in the context of purposeful writing
- making it possible for every child to contribute
- providing reading material relevant to the child's own experiences
- starting where the children are: books about us, what we do and know
- providing published stories as models
- making composing easier by making sure ideas already exist through discussion in the group
- helping children to gain control of language through the process of creating their own shared text
- exposing children to different language forms so that they become aware of how things are said in written language
- giving emotional support
- retelling stories so children learn to control their structure
- helping children work their contributions into a coherent whole, a unified story
- extending, revising and improving on what has been written, editing and publishing with support of peers and adults
- sitting down and writing alongside the children to provide a model
- providing a 'workshop' environment where children learn to write by writing
- providing opportunities for children to make their own labels, captions, signs to enhance their play
- working towards a confident and independent child, fostering an understanding and readiness to see how reading and writing work and building on it
- making them confident that what they offer is acceptable
- talking/discussing/conferencing with child - *At the core of the conference is a teacher asking a child to teach her about the subject* (Donald Graves)
- discussing with the children about their writing but leaving the responsibility for the writing in their hands

- a collaborative process between teacher and children, and between children
- the teacher enabling children to develop and organise their ideas

Ideas for shared writing

Telling stories children know: traditional, favourite stories.

Extending stories they know.

Creating new stories and poems.

Creating texts around school activities - posters for sports day, reports on topic work.

Planning structured play activities

- listing requirements for creating a clinic, cafe, cinema, post office, supermarket
- making signs and displays
- advertising for items parents might be able to provide

Rewriting songs, poems, games, nursery rhymes etc. and perhaps substituting new words that still rhyme.

Writing up information for the day - *Hayley is 5 years old today.*

Writing captions, notices, lists, menus, shopping lists, lists of names, words beginning with 'A' or words with an 'A' in them.

Sending letters, invitations composed together.

How to share writing in practice

Use an easel or rostrum with the teacher acting as scribe.

Use large (long) sheets of paper on the floor or table.

Write alongside children.

Observe and respond to children.

Arrange small group discussions and then encourage the children to write.

Provide a variety of writing materials: clip boards, paper, order forms, paper, pens, felt pens and so on.

What results?

Children become confident writers and don't feel it's a hard skill to obtain.

Children become apprentices working alongside an experienced writer.

Language and ideas offered by the children are considered by teachers and other children, then shaped and reshaped before the final draft and publication.

Children experience the process of creating a text or book, as authors and illustrators.

The conventions of print, ie letters, words, spacing, punctuation, left to right page organisation, mistakes, top to bottom, are made explicit by the teacher in her role as scribe.

The children see the purpose of writing.

Children become aware of different forms of writing.

Children get a sense of story structure.

As writers of different texts children develop a sense of audience.

Children are involved in decision making.

Reading materials relevant to the child's own needs are developed.

Rita Collison, Debbie Gillet, Gayner Moorhouse and Anne Wilson, Manchester Writing Project

Reading, talking and writing

A pre-school child develops a natural whole language, functional, real and relevant. Children begin their language learning at home with listening and talk in a relaxed atmosphere, where the smallest steps along the way are applauded and encouraged. They feel secure and are willing to take risks. Language learning from an early age begins as a whole. A single word uttered by a baby can carry within it a wealth of meaning. A few scribbles on a piece of paper can represent a long and interesting story. Many authentic literacy experiences — real opportunities to listen, talk, read and write — occur at home and in the community. Schools sometimes isolate language learning from these meaning-based experiences, and divide the language programme into separate parts in order to simplify the process. Don Holdaway talks about the 'dismembering of the literacy process'[4] Activities that involve fragments discourage pupils and hinder risk-taking, and often prevent the exchange of ideas.

From the beginning of the National Writing Project, the value of linking talk and reading has been emphasised. Most text becomes clearer in meaning if talk precedes the task of reading. The talk may be between children, or between teacher and child.

A key concept which seems to bring these ideas together is that of dialogue. Until quite recently, accounts of children's language learning have focused on individual children, cataloguing all that they said or wrote and assuming that such language could be divorced from the context in which it arose.

But it is clear from observing children at home and at school that children are not just doing exercises in language learning, but are engaged in perceiving and interpreting the social context and generating hypotheses about how language is used within social contexts. They make hypotheses about writing through watching other writers, talking about writing, reading, and talking about print. This is how they work out the ground rules for writing in their particular culture.[5/6]

An illustration of how much young children have already learned about writing when they come to school and how, through dialogue, they can develop as writers comes from an often quoted pair of reception children in Sheila Hughes' class in Shropshire.

Critical readers and writers

Fiona and Neil were invited by their teacher to help each other to write once a week for six weeks, starting with stories about their favourite colours. Fiona wrote her story herself with the teacher providing some spellings; Neil dictated his story for the teacher to write. Each text was accompanied by a picture. Once a week they exchanged books and made comments which the teacher wrote underneath. The following extracts demonstrate how much each child knew about the requirements of a text, and how much influence children can have on each other's development as critical readers and writers.

Week 1

Fiona wrote:	*'I like black because I have a toy black dog and I have always wanted a real life black dog.'*
Neil commented:	*'She could have made it better if she'd put legs on the dog.'*
Neil wrote:	*'I like yellow wallpaper and I am going to ask my dad if I can have some.'*
Fiona commented:	*'He should have put "wallpaper" at the end of his story.'*

Week 2

Fiona wrote:	*'Red makes my Mummy happy. She has a red Renault 5 car and there is a lot of room in the boot.'*

---

[4] D. Holdaway: *The Foundations of Literacy* (Ashton Scholastic)
[5] G. Wells: *The Meaning Makers* (Hodder & Stoughton)
[6] B. Tizard & M. Hughes: *Young Children Learning* (Fontana)

Neil commented:	*'She should have put spokes on the wheels and two lights front and back.'*
Neil wrote:	*'This is a red lorry and I like it.'*
Fiona commented:	*'He should have said where the lorry was going and why he liked it.'*

By Week 6

Fiona wrote:	*'The bear is trying to get some honey out of a tree. He looks very cuddly but really he is dangerous.'*
Neil commented:	*'Draw a bigger tree. It is a good story.'*
Neil wrote:	*'My teddy bear is sitting by a tree thinking about doing something naughty.'*
Fiona commented:	*'Ears and paws on the bear. I would like to know what naughty thing this teddy was going to do.'*

Fiona and Neil, through their partnership, have clearly learned from each other about how to respond critically to another's writing. Their writing also seems to indicate the effect such critical readership can have on writing. Compare, for instance, Neil's first text with his text six weeks later.

Shropshire Writing Project

Reading for writing

Sharing books with children is an important contributory factor in their development as writers. In our nursery we try to spend as much time as possible reading stories, talking about the way books work and looking closely at the different forms of illustrations and print. The children come to understand the many different styles and techniques used by authors and illustrators, and their growing awareness of book conventions influences the way they approach their own writing.

Children's writing is often a straightforward reflection of books that they know well and have shared often with adults or peers.

Juliana

Many of the above examples have illustrated the strong influence of reading on children's development as writers. Thus, different models of writing have a powerful effect on children's choices about how to write. We need to look not only at the types of material available, but also at the status we give to the texts. What is read aloud; what is not? What goes on the wall; what does not? What is valued for boys and what for girls? Which languages are represented; which are not?

This account provides some powerful observations on the relationship between reading and writing.

In Juliana's example both the text and illustrations were taken directly from the book.

The following example was produced at the time of Halloween:

Hang

Clearly, Meg and Owl are the central characters in this illustration, and were derived from a book being used in the classroom. Hang then added her own script as the accompanying text.

Many of the stories we share with children contain minute details that would often be missed in just one reading, or if the book were only shared with the whole class. Sharing stories in small groups encourages a growing awareness of the importance of illustrations.

David

David's picture shows an awareness of detail and of the importance of written information, such as the number of the church and the writing on the side of the car.

Whole class project books also demonstrate children's perception that written material is as important as other visual evidence. We kept a book of drawings showing the development of our frogspawn. Most of the children drew or painted pictures of the different stages in the frog's life cycle. Other children also referred to reference books and decided to include written information with their drawings.

In Juliana's piece of work, the dietary requirements of the frog are laid out for each stage of its development:

Juliana

One of the most significant developments is the children's growing awareness that the text and illustrations can reinforce each other.

In the next example, Tijen and Caron demonstrate their awareness that print and illustrations both help to tell a story. It is particularly interesting to note that the two children worked together. One child did the illustrating and the other wrote the text (which is often the case in the making of published materials). Another interesting point was that the two children used their story as a proper reading book. It was taken home and read to other children and adults in our classroom.

She is watching the birds.

Tijen and Caron

Book material, then, has a clear influence on children's writing. The children use the ideas contained in books and quickly adopt a bookish layout. They constantly refine their ideas and skills in the process of making their own books. At first their own books are often fairly exact copies (both illustrations and print). Next comes a tendency to refine the illustrations and use their own print. Later still, both illustrations and print are more independently produced.

These examples show that exposure to a variety of real books influences the way in which children write. They learn about book conventions and about different ways of presenting text and illustrations. Good reading material must encourage good writers, and by giving children different models of writing we can expect to receive a more varied written output.

Steve Cummings, Grinling Gibbons School, ILEA

Developing a language policy

Teachers within their own classrooms have become researchers of the whole language approach. This reception class teacher describes how she is developing her policy on writing and illustrates the results.

As a teacher of top Juniors for ten years, I had often taught children who were reluctant to write anything down on paper because they couldn't spell a word or didn't know precisely what to write. When I changed to the Infant reception class, this reluctance to write, this fear of making mistakes, was in my mind as I planned the year's work. I decided to make some changes in standard Infant practice in relation to writing.

My reception class consisted of the younger half of that year's intake, children who were four years old but would not be five until late in the school year. They were from many different cultural and linguistic backgrounds. I decided, first, to concentrate on oral work and drawing to aid language development. I gave them very many opportunities to talk about their family, and the activities they did before and after they came to school. Lots of action rhymes were sung, and I read them a great many stories. I asked the children to draw pictures of things that we had talked about and then went round talking to the children about their drawings. Some just named the objects on the page, while other children talked more fully. While they watched, I simply wrote down what they said, using lower case letters, with capitals only for names, and then read it back to them. At the end of the session we shared the work as a class. The children were never asked or expected to copy under my writing.

I was deliberately presenting the idea that writing is for reading, whether it was my writing by their pictures, my writing around the classroom, writing in books, writing in the environment, or the children's own first attempts to shape letters.

By the middle of the second term I was confident that the majority of the children could make a good attempt at writing all the letters of the alphabet and were ready to move on to writing words and phrases. One day, without preamble, I simply asked them to write their names on their worksheets. The majority of the class could do so; the children who didn't write their name correctly, wrote a group of letters of about the same length as their name, including some of the correct letters.

Encouraged by this result, a few days later I asked the children to draw a picture of their own choice and write about it. They all attempted this without question and I asked them to read what they had written to me. The results were varied. There were words copied from around the room, words memorised from reading books and from television (*A-team*, *Robin Hood*), even some complete sentences. The least advanced children simply wrote lower case letters, but these were arranged across the page in lines from left to right. One of these early attempts is shown here:

'My car is like silver'

At the pre-reading stage we give children access to books, and accept that they will chatter away to themselves, imitating in their own terms adults reading stories. Perhaps the same principle should be applied to the early stages of writing. I feel we should not devalue the experiments of the young child by classifying early attempts at writing as mere scribble, or inaccurate copying. If writing is always presented as something to read, and if visual memory, letter formation and phonic awareness are being developed alongside reading experience, children's confidence and competence as *writers and readers* will develop simultaneously.

Joyce Emsen, St. James' C. of E. Primary School, Birmingham

3 The developing writer

In this section, we look at ways in which children's writing can develop in a supportive partnership between home and school.

Young children arrive at school with different understandings, experiences and expectations. Sensitive teachers give children time and opportunity to experiment and develop their own language awareness, interweaving talking, listening, mark-making and reading; taking time to look carefully at each child's perception of writing; providing a rich and stimulating writing environment. Young children need to develop a positive attitude, seeing themselves as writers from the beginning.

Watch out for development

These examples of reception and middle Infants speculating about sea-horses show that children have different perceptions about writing, and about their own ability to use the written word as a means of communication.

Frogwell County Primary School, Chippenham, Wiltshire

As teachers, we need to be aware of the wide variety of children's personal experiences of writing, so that we can more appropriately encourage them to take on the task of writing for themselves, refining their early efforts as they develop a greater knowledge of how writing works.

We have seen how teachers who make appropriate provision, space and time for writing help children to write for widening purposes and audiences in an increasing variety of formats.

If we are to support this provision with an understanding of what children know about writing, we need to give ourselves time to build up our knowledge of children's writing processes and of what they already know about writing. Using these observations, we can decide how best to help each child's confidence and competence to develop.

Expectations and opportunities

A key question teachers have asked about writing development is *'What are our expectations for the developing writer?'*

Among the expectations included are:

- to be a risk-taker — willing to experiment with new writing forms and functions

- to be a collaborator — developing a piece of writing through discussion and negotiation with others

- to be a responder — developing a critical response to one's own writing by being a critical reader of others' texts

- to be a confident writer, aware of one's achievements and limitations

- to be able to select an appropriate form for a piece of writing (a letter, a poem, a list)

- to be able to revise and adapt the structure of the text according to its audience and purpose

- to be able to use editorial skills: correcting spelling, punctuation and grammar

- to be able to use writing for learning, for the formulation of ideas

Any attempt to set age groups against these expectations produces great problems. Experience of different types and styles of writing will lead to improved writing, but the process is not a linear one.

If we look carefully at children's work with these principles in mind, we begin to build up a picture of children's understanding of the written language and how they see themselves as writers.

These pieces of work are by children aged about five years. They give a sample of the rich variety of knowledge about writing that young children already have when they begin formal education.

Saiqa wrote in a notebook in the classroom 'café'. She used two differently coloured felt-tip pens as she wrote in the language forms she was aware of — Urdu/Arabic and English.

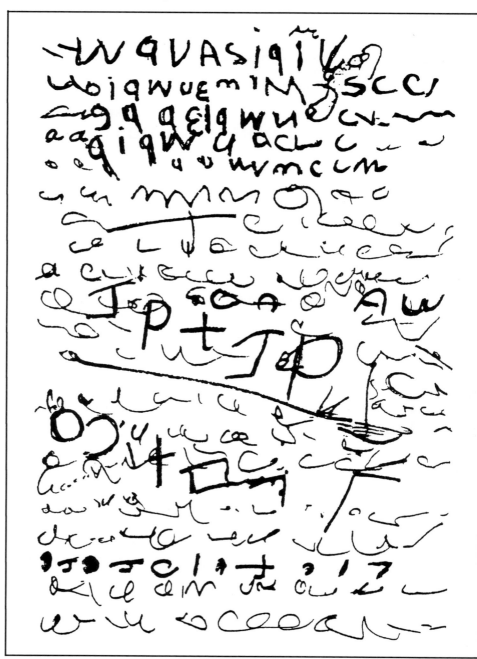

Saiqa

Rachael was well aware that her writing carried messages. In her book about Father Christmas, written in several sessions, she dictated her meaning to an adult. This flowing and varied language was then written underneath Rachael's own writing. Rachael had a clear view of the orientation of print too, if necessary rearranging her text to surround the illustrations, as she had seen in story books.

Rachael

Naomi, writing in the home corner, showed that she understood the different purposes of letters and numerals, and that writing is a means of communication with absent friends. Her letter to a cousin was placed in an envelope, carrying the address.

Naomi

Arzoo wrote this when she was part of a small group of children drawing and writing about their homes and activities.

Arzoo

> I Stm mumtwc

She wrote carefully, forming her letters accurately and working from left to right: *'I said to my mum, it was cold.'* Initial letters represent most of the words, but she also included two words that she could write from memory.

Sandra had made her picture of 'Mr Sandy' by drawing with a sticky brush, then shaking sand over the work. An adult asked her how she had made him, so she offered to write out instructions for making such pictures.

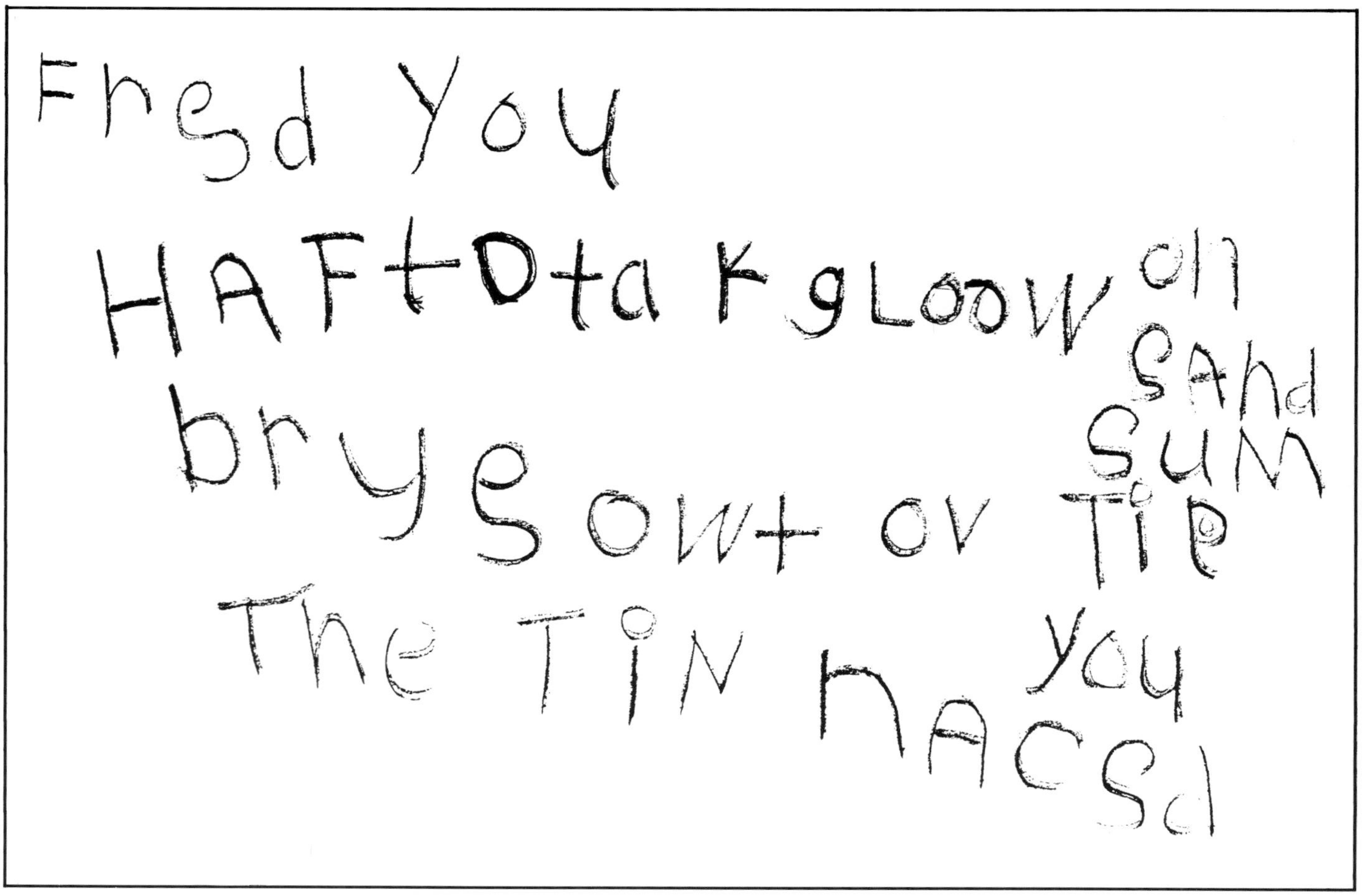

> Fresd you
> HAFtOta rgLooW oll sand
> brysowt ov Tie sum
> The Tin naccd you

Sandra

'First, you have to take (the) glue brush out of the tin. Next you tip some sand on.'

She was confident of the arrangement of words on the page, initially working from top to bottom and left to right, and had an ingenious way of dealing with lack of space on her paper.

Claire's class had been reading and talking about nursery rhymes. It was suggested to one group of children that they might like to write to someone from a rhyme and help them with their problems. A lot of talk and laughter followed, as they discussed the predicaments of Little Boy Blue, Bo Peep etc.

Claire, who wasn't usually a very enthusiastic writer, set to work with a will to send this reassuring letter to the 'little kittens':

Claire

'Dear little kittens,
I have found your mittens in the box. Collect them at the Mulberry Bush at 2 p.m.
Bye-bye
Love Claire'

She had an excellent grasp of the purpose of her message and of the accepted format for letters.

The information that we collect in this way can be used to help us to:

- assess and monitor the children's knowledge and development as writers
- examine our strategies for encouraging this development to take place
- check on the suitability and range of writing provision and tasks made available to the children

- keep careful, well annotated notes and records of the children's development

Cleveland and Manchester Writing Projects

One child's development

One of the Project co-ordinators kept a detailed record of one child, Christopher. Some extracts from her case study demonstrate the kind of observation that can help the teacher to monitor development. For each piece of writing, a brief record is kept of the immediate context, but this needs to be read alongside a description of the whole writing environment. Such a picture is necessarily subjective, but it can indicate what is being valued by the teacher and what messages about literacy are intended to be conveyed to the children.

The observations about each of Christopher's texts concentrate on his achievements - what he has learned about writing. Obviously, many of these focus on the acquisition of the writing system itself: letter shapes, spelling, orientation of text. However, these achievements need to be seen in relation to the choices he has made about the content: what topic he writes about, what he chooses to represent about a particular topic, how he organises the text around the page. These choices about subject and form indicate significant knowledge about his literacy culture. For example, his choice of characters like Batman and the Incredible Hulk reflect strong gender-related choices, and his use of story structure reflects a bias towards story books in his early reading experiences. The literacy profile of any one child is multifaceted and cannot be rendered down to a simple set of skills or benchmarks.

Two months before his fifth birthday, Christopher moved from a short time in a nursery class to a vertically grouped class of four-and-a-half to six-year-olds.

He is the elder of two children, living on a large estate in an industrial area. His parents were proud of his interest in books and in his drawings, but rather critical of the fact that he had not yet begun to write. They had taught him to recognise letter shapes and letter names.

Christopher loved to draw, to make models with construction equipment and to read to himself. His new teacher encouraged these interests and Christopher often told his favourite stories to her, following the storyline accurately and with enthusiasm, and using a great deal of 'book language'. She showed him how to follow print with his finger and began to heighten his awareness of how the story's message is carried in the print, as well as in the illustrations. She also wrote labels and captions to accompany some of his models and drawings, although Christopher would not attempt this for himself.

The classroom was arranged so that the children could move freely from activity to activity, being encouraged to concentrate fully on one activity before choosing a different one. Books and writing equipment were always available for individual use. More formalised reading and writing work took place in small groups, but the children were encouraged to try to write for themselves at every opportunity. They were not asked to 'copywrite'.

A small group of children shared *The Three Bears* with their teacher, looking at the illustrations and text together. Christopher liked this story and often read it for himself. Later, he took this drawing to his teacher:

The teacher talked about the drawing with Christopher, and then asked him to write the characters' names. After some hesitation, he did this, asking the teacher only how to write the letter *G*.

What does he know about writing?

that pictures can represent story characters

that writing usually moves across the page from left to right

that words appear in straight lines and are separate from one another

that signs (letters) can represent sounds and that a combination of these signs makes a word

that some sounds are represented by more than one sign; in *'taniy'*, he makes a sensible assumption/guess that the word will end in *y*, but perhaps he also knows that *i* sometimes represents the same sound

the accurate shape of a range of capital letters

On another occasion, Christopher's teacher asked a group of children to illustrate their favourite nursery rhyme. She intended to accompany these by writing out the rhymes (alongside) herself, but Christopher wrote his own version of 'Humpty

Dumpty' quite unaided. Later, he asked his teacher to write out the rhyme correctly — the first time he had acknowledged the difference between his writing and that of adults.

What does he know about writing?

- that rhymes are arranged in a particular way on the page

- that print usually starts at the top of the page and moves downwards

- how to write a large range of capital and lower case letters

- how to represent each sound in a word with a letter, although he occasionally uses one letter only to stand for a whole word, eg *K* for *'King's'* and *s* for *'sat'*.

- that words carry a consistent phonic pattern — *ol* is used to represent *'all'* in *'fall'* and *'all'*

- how to hold a long piece of text in his head as he writes

What experiences were available to support Christopher's reading and writing?

- Books — fiction, poetry, non-fiction — were freely available in the classroom and children were positively encouraged to read them.

- Stories were frequently read to small groups of children, every day.

- Nursery rhymes, songs and poems were used as valuable reading resources.

- Models, activities and paintings were labelled or had captions added to them. Children were encouraged to write these for themselves.

- Adults acted as scribes for groups of children as they worked on stories and accounts.

- Older children worked on story drafts with their teacher.

- Alphabet books and friezes were part of the classroom environment and were used for reading and discussion. Some were made by the class.

- Notes were exchanged with other classes and teachers.

- 'Feelie' letters and magnetic letters were available for handling and use.

- Books were made in class, and became part of the class book provision.

- Books were taken home to be read there.

- Children were consistently encouraged to write for themselves, for their own purposes, and did so in an increasingly confident way.

- Writing was used to support and develop role-play and to record factual information.

- Children and adults shared one another's writing.

- Children read to one another and shared texts when listening to taped stories.

- Dictionaries, word banks and alphabet books were used often by the children.

About three weeks later, this piece of work was found in the class writing area after school. Christopher had completed it there, but had not shown it to an adult nor, as he usually did, taken it home. The drawing is typical, as he frequently depicted themes of fantasy and violence, but the text was the first example of sustained imaginative writing he had been seen to produce.

Next day, he read the text to his teacher: *'The hulk is going to destroy Beastman with Batman.'*

What does he know about writing?

- where words begin and end and that, conventionally, we separate words by a space

- that two letters can represent one sound as in *'wish'* or *'with'*

- some conventional spellings — *'man'* and *'is'*

He was also making choices about subject matter. We can already see preferences in his writing which appear to be gender-marked. Questions need to be raised about the influences on such choices: what reading materials are available; what he sees to be valued behaviour for boys, and so on.

As part of a group project, several children wrote and illustrated parts of the Nativity story. The children had read several versions of the story and these had been available in the classroom for private reading. Christopher had been particularly interested in Jan Pienkowski's *Christmas,* and his illustrations for the class book showed that he had been influenced by Pienkowski's work.

This writing was done quickly, with no help from other children or adults, although there had been considerable discussion of which part of the story each child would write. Christopher chose to relate the most fearful part of the story:

the inshl. cums to teu The diffint pipl That theey HAFTo asclyp from cig Herd WAYL cig HeID wosnt Wochin so Tey hed Tuw escp Tuw Tey cun

'The angel comes to tell the different people that they have to escape from King Herod while King Herod wasn't watching so they had to escape to their country.'

What does he know about writing?

- conventional arrangement of words

- more lower case letters than previously seen in his work

- complex sentence and text structure

- a more consistent representation of digraphs — *'the', 'theey', 'wochin'*

Six weeks later, with a new teacher, the class was asked to write about their weekend activities. Some children now used personal word books to establish correct spellings, but Christopher continued to work at his own rapidly developing knowledge of spelling conventions.

M.l Febrwdry
LaSTNayT I weNt to
MY NaNLiNs IPLiD
ALiTL Gim · AFT I
HaD PLiD TOW·dwr NaN
FraNsis cIm   ✱ MY
NaN FraNsis PromisT
The✱AT I cuD Go to
The Pichs I WeNT
to   MY HaWs I puT
oN MY CuWT I WeNT
To my Na✱Ns to aSC
iF dWr GraNDAD woNTb to

CuM· to oNe HuDreD aND ✱iDaL
MiShesNs hE SAD No ThNk
Yuw So TheN wiY weNT To
oNe HuNDroaNDoNe Da L✱MiShiNS
FeST MisTMGuw cim·oN
aFT ThaT ✱ooa✱N DiDaLiShNS
cIm oN ·

'Last night I went to my Nan Lyn's. I played a little game. After I had played two, our Nan Frances came. My Nan Frances promised that I could go to the pictures. I went to my house. I put on my coat. I went to my Nan's to ask if our Grandad wanted to come to "101 Dalmatians". He said "No thank you" so then we went to "101 Dalmatians". First "Mr Magoo" came on. After that, "101 Dalmatians" came on.'

What does he know about writing?

- his account is well sequenced and detailed

- he has another try if he is not happy with his spelling

- he has a greater awareness of more complex letter combinations — *'dalmishens' (dalmatians), 'yuw' (you) 'mistmguw' (Mr Magoo), 'nayt' (night), 'baws' (house) 'cuwt' (coat)*

- he seems quite clear where words begin and end

- he uses a wide range of conventionally spelled words

- he is consistent in working out representations of similar sounds eg the use of *i* in *'gim' (game)*, *'plid' (played)*, *'cim' (came)*, *'dalmishins' (dalmatians)*; *aw* is used in both *'awr' (our)* and *'haws' (house)*

- he shows some awareness of punctuation marks

- he uses appropriate linking words and phrases — *'after I had played'*; *'to ask if'*; *'so then'*

- he uses both reported and direct speech

What experiences were available to support Christopher's reading and writing?

- The class continued to take pleasure in reading and drawing, model making and painting, constructional activities and writing.

- Christopher regularly watched *Words and Pictures* on television (at home and at school), showing an interest in both the stories and the highlighted sounds.

- The class played oral word and sound games, having fun with alliteration and rhymes.

- He was consciously reading the text of books, often wrestling alone with new stories and rarely asking for help.

- He read with adults regularly.

- Writing, in many formal and informal ways, was taking place all around him, with adults and children sharing and valuing one another's work.

- His parents had taken him to join a public library and were finding more opportunities for Christopher to write with them at home.

- He was part of many collaborative writing tasks and observed those of other children.

- Puzzles and games which develop an awareness of letter sounds and combinations were used with small groups.

In a classroom where literacy was given high priority, and adults shared a real enthusiasm for reading and writing, Christopher continued to develop confidence in his own abilities as a writer and a reader.

Margaret J. Meek, Cleveland Writing Project Co-ordinator

Writing is thinking

The description of Christopher's writing development emphasises the need to consider the context in which writing develops. While Christopher was developing the conventions of writing — spelling, spacing, letter shapes — he was making more significant developments in his understanding of the different forms of writing — poems, stories, descriptions — and their varying demands on his language resources. His growing control over different ways of writing reflected a context in which writing was used to reflect the child's thoughts, ideas and interests, and in which writing was firmly rooted in his experiences of reading and talk.

Some teachers of younger children feel they have become primarily teachers of the secretarial skills of spelling, handwriting and punctuation. Focusing children's attention on such aspects means that those narrow skills become *writing* to the children. Often, very little attention is paid to ways of encouraging children to write in order to communicate. Many children therefore have a narrow view of the purposes of writing. Young children frequently see it as a school activity only, with little relation to real life, done in order to please their teachers. They have little sense of writing as communication, nor of writing for personal pleasure; still less, of writing as a means of working out ideas, and expressing personal meaning.

> Dreams and nightmares
>
> I don't like having bad Dreams or even wosed of all nightmares. Sometimes there so bad I wake up and cry. Sometimes I want to wake up but I can't. Sometimes I forget them. Some peple have nice Dreams. I like some Dreams I have, very bad Dreams. Grown ups don't have bad Dreams much I don't think. In Dreams you some thinks reliy happening. I once thout some one was about to kill me. I think some one is outside my room because the floor bords squeak. Sometimes I think the wind is a monster.

A top Infant child in a Wiltshire school was asked to write what she thought about dreams and nightmares, as part of a topic on 'Night'.

She responded by considering the question, deliberating about it as she wrote.

A child of her age might have been expected to recall a dream or make up a nightmare, but this girl demonstrates a thoughtful response, in which she clarifies her opinions and is possibly helped to come to terms with her own night-time fears.

Jo Stone, Wiltshire Writing Project Co-ordinator, outlines five ways of helping children to see writing as thinking:

1 *Recollection* — where children are asked to write about what they already know or what they think they know about something.

2 *Consideration* — where children reflect or deliberate in forming an opinion.

3 *Formation* — where children form new thoughts.

4 *Speculation* — where children theorise by making a scientific guess, using observation and speculation.

5 *Examination* — where children think about problem-solving.

This example of formative writing shows the value of encouraging children to formulate questions to help their own learning. Four children, aged six to seven years, identified areas of interest about their favourite birds.

questions

why do Robins like winter?
how did the Robin get its name?

what other colours are there on its body
what colour is a young Robin?
were do you often see them?
what do they eat?

what cid of songs do they sing?
what colour are they babys?
Were do they build they nest?
how long does it tack til theycan fly?
What colour eggs? what cid of food?
Were is he found?

Christopher had been one of a group of children who had shopped for ingredients and made a class fruit salad. Later, the children and their teacher made a pictorial record entitled 'How we made a fruit salad', adding adult-scribed captions to each illustration. Christopher volunteered to write about the lemons, and quickly wrote as follows:

Another example of thinking through writing is given by Christopher, the Cleveland five-year-old referred to above.

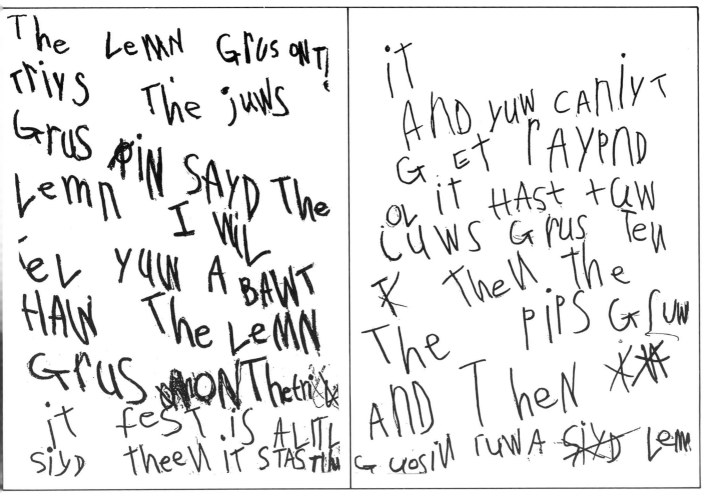

(Note: you need to read down the left-hand page and then up the right-hand one — an interesting solution to the problem of writing continuous texts.)

'The lemon grows on the trees. The juice grows inside the lemon. I will tell you about how the lemon grows on the tree. It first is a little seed. Then it starts growing into a lemon and then then pips grow. Then the juice grows then all it has to do to get ripened and you can eat it.'

Notice 'I will tell you about how the lemon grows'. Christopher often used phrases like this as though to clarify and order his own thoughts when describing or narrating a sequence.

There are numerous examples of a thoughtful approach to writing for young children, examples which show how opportunities to use writing for thinking have a value for all areas of the curriculum. They also provide an important personal function for writing, as the final example from Christopher illustrates.

Christopher loved to draw and write in his journal. One day, having been part of several class discussions where his teacher was concerned to emphasise that Christmas is a time for giving, as well as for receiving gifts, Christopher showed his journal to his mother at home time. He explained to her that there was a secret inside that he didn't want his sister to hear, so he'd written a message:

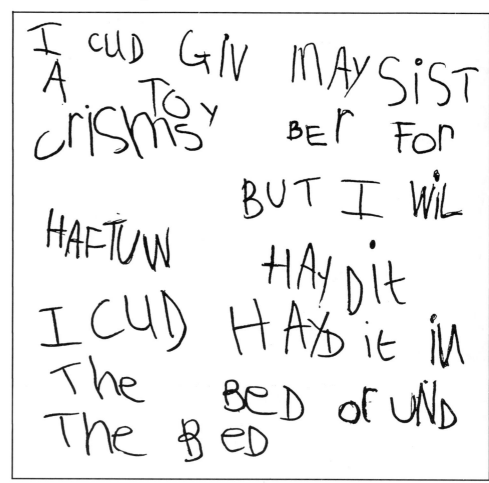

'I could give my sister a toy bear for Christmas but I will have to hide it. I could hide it in the bed or under the bed.'

Record keeping

In classrooms where children write solely on the instructions of the teacher, where early writing is in the form of 'writing under' teachers' sentences and where most of that work is done in an exercise book of one kind or another, observation of a child's progress presents few problems. However, in classrooms where children are encouraged to write independently; to write for a variety of audiences and purposes and in a variety of settings; to have control over the product (the how, the when and the where) so that public and private writing are an everyday part of the child's experience, keeping track of writing development can be more problematic.

Teachers in such classrooms are aware of the necessity to monitor each child's writing development in order to support it, and to offer help and encouragement where needed. Keeping good records is therefore vital, not only for the teacher's own information but also for parents and for other staff.

Since the writing is not necessarily collected by the teacher after a session — indeed, the child's personal writing may be taken home, passed on to a friend or thrown in the bin (and we cannot dispute this decision about its fate) — we may worry that important developments could be missed, developments that may only be tried out by the child when the writing is done in private. This could be in a 'writing centre' where materials are provided but the work is not set by the teacher. Steve Cummings (from Grinling Gibbons School, ILEA) suggests that the most important information is obtained by observation:

'Teachers can learn so much more from being with a child when the child is writing, than from getting a piece of writing after the child has finished it. You are more likely to spot a significant aspect in a child's writing development if you work alongside or with them.'

While this would seem the ideal way of monitoring development, it is helpful also to have samples of work to support such observation. It is extremely useful to keep a dated and annotated collection of each child's work as an ongoing record. This can be done by:

- maintaining individual folders, containing regular samples of the child's representational work — paintings, drawings, writing

- pinning individual named pockets on the classroom walls where children are encouraged to store their work and from which samples may be drawn at regular intervals, such samples forming the basis of the records

- keeping personal writing books as the main record, supplemented regularly by samples of other work

Concerns about a developmental approach

These examples of development and ways of monitoring it have illustrated the knowledge of writing that children demonstrate when provided with supportive classroom contexts. In discussions of such an approach to writing development, there are always a number of concerns raised by teachers about individual children, and about the control of writing conventions. Below, a few of these concerns are addressed.

What about the inhibited child?

To create an atmosphere where children will produce their own writing is not difficult with most young children, but with older children who have already learned to use word books or *Breakthrough* folders there may be a need to build confidence gradually. The principle of looking at what the child can do and what the child understands is most important. The child may be able to identify the initial letter of a word and find the right page in the word book, or may have memorised the position of a word in the *Breakthrough* folder. These strategies are both useful and important, not just for the stage the child is at now, but also for adult life (for example, when using a dictionary or locating a particular passage in a book). However, their usefulness at any stage is limited if they are the only strategies a child can use. The teacher's job is to extend the child's understandings, point out new possibilities, and reduce the reliance on a single method of approaching writing.

The most serious obstacle to progress in writing is the development in the young writer of a fear of failure. This fear of getting it wrong will ultimately lead to a reluctance to face the task at all. Unless children take risks and are willing to make errors, their progress in writing will be slow. Children who are willing to invent spellings for words usually become fluent writers in the process. The question of whether or not a child is a risk-taker depends on a number of factors including personality, parental expectation and the classroom environment.

By attaching value to the message rather than the surface features (handwriting and spelling) of the writing, we take away the pressure of 'getting it right'. One way to help take away this pressure is by giving children a book in which they can express their thoughts, feelings or ideas without any outside pressures. The following was written by a middle Infant child, who was initially very inhibited:

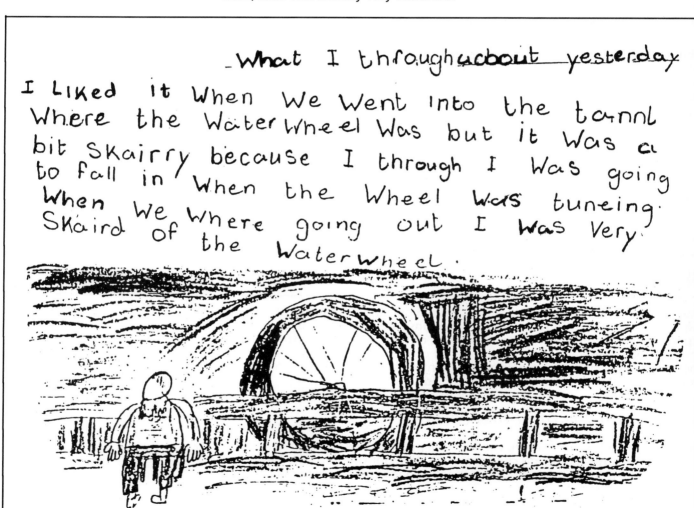

Another successful 'way in' with inhibited children is the picture planning approach. The following story was written by three children from a reception Infant class. After talking about their favourite fairy tales, the children were asked to fold their paper into four equal parts to plan the story.

'Once upon a time there was three little pigs and a dinosaur. The three little pigs killed the dinosaur. If you're wondering why they killed him it was because he was going to eat them.'

The reluctant writer may also be helped by a simple device: the 'magic line'. Lucy Scott-Ashe from the Avon Writing Project describes this:

'If children are not confident enough to "have a go at spelling", then the "magic line" can be a useful way of helping them to write independently.'

The teacher tells the children that if they do not know how to spell a word they can put a line instead. Some children's first piece of writing may very well look like this! A line is used to represent each word.

'My baby brother is sweet. Me and my sister like playing with him.'

Do not be daunted! If this is the case, it is time to suggest that the child puts in the first letter of the word whenever possible. The writing may now look like this:

'I went BMXing. It was fun.'

When the child is working confidently, the teacher should encourage him/her to add other letters and, with encouragement, have a go at spelling.

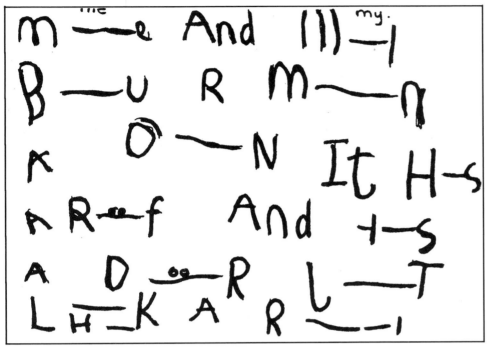

'Me and my brother are making a den. It has a roof and has a door just like a real house.'

Where parents object to the word 'magic', the line could be called something else, such as a 'spelling line'.

The advantages of this technique are:

1 The children are able to write down their ideas without help from the teacher.

2 The teacher is free to move around the classroom and talk to the children about their work. (S)he no longer has to spend time writing in word books.

All the strategies mentioned in Section Two should also be appropriate for helping reluctant writers to make a start.

What about spelling?

The following sheet attempts to summarise some of the points of development to recognise in children's spelling, and some of the strategies which can support early spelling explorations.

Teachers in the National Writing Project are supported by research in their belief that children learn to spell by writing, inventing spellings, and refining their understanding of print.

Spelling needs attention, but not at the composing stage. Children need to acquire spelling independence with responsibility for their own proof reading. Invented spelling makes diagnosis of the child's rules for spelling possible. Spelling instructions should follow conferring about the content of the writing.

Begin with the children. Observe carefully. What does each one understand about writing? Now think about these possibilities...

NaN MIN9 otFh ag

Pre-phonemic speller

Role-modelling by teacher scribing. Surround with print lists, reminders, 'thank you' letters, instructions, labels, messages, diaries, cards, signs.

Free activities on paper with a variety of implements – materials, sand, clay, paint, plasticine, sparkles, sawdust, blackboard, finger paints.

Flood with good quality books, catalogues, own writing.

ЭHs NPWS RKL Is LPP

Phonemic speller

Role-modelling by teacher scribing.

Phonic games, *Pictogram* alphabet, *Letterland;* 'writing corner' – creating banks, offices, Post Offices, newspaper offices, cafés.

Tracing blends, spelling patterns.

the seyhos has a Kulle tail
and spiks oluvu It has it got a mot

Transitional speller

Word banks, trying-out books, selected spellings for the individual to work on, spelling strategies, look – cover – write – check, family groups.

Spelling patterns and rules: full stops, apostrophes, capitalisation, suffixes, letter blends, dictionaries.

An overview

It is not easy to summarise a collection such as this, drawing as it does on the experiences of teachers all over Britain. Moreover, we want to avoid giving a 'blueprint' for classroom practice, as what is successful for one group of children may not be so for another.

This section attempts, though, to put together some of the main strands which together seem to summarise effective classroom practices for developing writing in the early years.

Observe carefully:

- Make opportunities to observe individual children to see how they approach writing.

- Talk with small groups or individuals, to establish a clear view of their perceptions of writing and their ability to write.

- Decide which strategies suit the writing needs of children.

- Find ways of keeping records of the children's achievements.

Provide good writing models:

- Use published work for discussion, to draw attention to the detail of style, arrangement on the page, punctuation.

- Write in front of the children, talking about what you are doing and why.

- Invite other writers into the classroom.

- Talk about why we like what we like.

- Frequently draw attention to letter sounds and how they are used in writing words.

- Provide, and use, varied and plentiful examples of different writing scripts and types.

- Develop the classroom as a word source.

Write for a variety of audiences:

- Encourage the feeling that a real audience gives the writer a purpose for writing.

- Consider letter writing for a purpose — one which will elicit a reply.

- Use audiences easily available in school — the cook, the lollipop lady, other children.

- Make writing equipment available as part of the class shop, home corner, hairdressers, travel agent or office.

- Develop class topics by enlarging your audience.

Teach planning:

- Encourage group or paired discussion of writing.

- Show the children, working as a group, how to make brief notes.

- Brainstorm as a group.

- Draft, and redraft, together, with the adult acting as a scribe, making mistakes, rewriting, rearranging.

- Make lists or 'starbursts' of ideas and vocabulary.

- Encourage children to write questions which clarify their thoughts.

- Make explicit the fact that writing may be a way of thinking on paper and is not always for sharing.
- Keep planning notes together — perhaps in a special folder — for reference.

Develop group work:

- Use a group approach to generate ideas and vocabulary for writing.
- Teach small groups to talk through a piece of writing — before, during and after its execution — and to act on their comments.
- Tape-record discussion to encourage a flow of ideas when children are freed from the writing task.
- Act as a scribe, to make notes and/or write up the drafts.
- Use separate articles from individual children to contribute to a class story or newspaper.

Build the children's confidence:

- Foster an attitude of 'having a go' at new/difficult words.
- Respond to their writing as a reader.
- Give children control over what they write.
- Devise strategies to help fluency, such as using the initial sound or a magic line to represent an unknown word, picturing words in their minds, circling words which worry them.
- Write alongside small groups of children, talking together about what you are doing.
- Help children to see other children and adults as part of the writing partnership, sharing in the process.
- Create an atmosphere where children know their best effort will be valued.
- Allow children to plan and write in their home language.
- Provide adequate time for talk, planning, thinking, doodling.

Encourage personal writing:

- Make a 'writing corner' in the classroom, where a variety of writing equipment is readily available.
- Encourage the purposeful use of such areas by working there yourself.
- Provide attractive notebooks to be used as personal journals/think books.
- Make class time for using these notebooks when everyone writes for personal purposes. Join in.
- Share your personal work with the children sometimes.
- Value writing in languages (and scripts) other than English.

Provide real purposes for writing:

- Write letters — as part of a project, to sick friends, to ask questions, to invite and thank visitors.
- Make books to supplement the class stocks.
- Contribute to the school/class magazine, joke book, newspaper.
- Fill in borrowing slips at the school library.

Record dialogues for home-made plays, puppet shows.

• Make shopping lists before cooking and write up recipes for a class book.

Keep a personal or class diary.

Record the birds which visit your bird table.

• Write instructions for making or using models.

Make labelled plans before building with the bricks or in the sand.

Encourage working with a partner:

Show how positive discussion of work can lead to plans for its development.

Prove that two heads are better than one when looking for spelling and organisational errors.

• Teach children to read their drafts to one another and work out how to improve them.

• Demonstrate early plans for writing which begin with a shared drawing, notes or a diagram.

• Encourage written response to a partner's work.

Vary the formats used:

• Plan projects or topics so that a variety of writing types will be needed.

• Encourage writing for planning and developing other classroom activities — model making, scientific observation, interviewing.

• Provide an array of different formats: application forms, letters, comics, posters.

Give public value to the children's writing:

• Use the posters, letters, invitations and jokes that the children write.

• Publish children's stories in attractively bound books which take their place in the book corner.

• Read aloud and display a variety of children's writing.

• Use children's work as a model for discussion.

Help them see writing as a process:

• Promote shared effort with collaborator or response partner.

• Teach and encourage careful checking, reorganising, redrafting.

• Value ideas and process as highly as the end product.

• Boost the children's confidence; free them from acting as composer and secretary simultaneously.

Above all — have confidence in the children, remembering that we learn to write by writing.

References and resources

The last fifteen years have seen the publication of many books and articles which provide insights into classroom practice, and frameworks for looking at the theories underlying the practice. A full list is impossible, but below are some of the sources which teachers in the Project have cited as useful in the development of their thinking. It goes without saying that the list would ideally include the hundreds of children's books which have influenced the teachers' work.

J.S. Bruner: *Actual Minds, Possible Worlds* (Harvard Educational Press 1986)

M. Clay: *What Did I Write?* (Heinemann 1975)

E. Ferreiro, A. Teberosky: *Literacy before Schooling* (Heinemann 1979)

H. Goelman, A. Oberg, F. Smith (ed.): *Awakening to Literacy* (Heinemann 1984)

N. Hall: *The Emergence of Literacy* (Hodder and Stoughton 1987)

D. Holdaway: *The Foundations of Literacy* (Ashton Scholastic 1979)

J. Newman: *The Craft of Children's Writing* (Scholastic 1984)

K. Perera: *Children's Writing and Reading* (Basil Blackwell 1984)

M. Spencer: 'Emergent literacies: a site for analysis' from *Language Arts 63 (5)* 1986

C.A. Temple, R.G. Nathan, N.A. Burris: *The Beginnings of Writing* (Allyn and Bacon 1982)

B. Tizard, M. Hughes: *Young Children Learning* (Fontana 1984)

G. Wells: *The Meaning Makers* (Hodder and Stoughton 1987)